Eva Panger

Hispanic Influence on American English

Eva Panger

Hispanic Influence on American English

Historical, Linguistic, Literary Aspects and Second Language Learning Process

VDM Verlag Dr. Müller

Imprint

Bibliographic information by the German National Library: The German National Library lists this publication at the German National Bibliography; detailed bibliographic information is available on the Internet at http://dnb.d-nb.de.

Any brand names and product names mentioned in this book are subject to trademark, brand or patent protection and are trademarks or registered trademarks of their respective holders. The use of brand names, product names, common names, trade names, product descriptions etc. even without a particular marking in this works is in no way to be construed to mean that such names may be regarded as unrestricted in respect of trademark and brand protection legislation and could thus be used by anyone.

Cover image: www.purestockx.com

Publisher:
VDM Verlag Dr. Müller Aktiengesellschaft & Co. KG, Dudweiler Landstr. 125 a, 66123 Saarbrücken, Germany,
Phone +49 681 9100-698, Fax +49 681 9100-988,
Email: info@vdm-verlag.de

Copyright © 2008 VDM Verlag Dr. Müller Aktiengesellschaft & Co. KG and licensors
All rights reserved. Saarbrücken 2008
2. Auflage

Produced in USA and UK by:
Lightning Source Inc., La Vergne, Tennessee, USA
Lightning Source UK Ltd., Milton Keynes, UK
BookSurge LLC, 5341 Dorchester Road, Suite 16, North Charleston, SC 29418, USA

ISBN: 978-3-639-02059-5

CONTENTS

HISTORICAL BACKGROUND 5

    1.1   Statistics 6

    1.2   The role of the Spanish language in daily life............................. 6

    1.3   Historical, cultural issues... 8

    1.4   Anglicism – influence of English on the South American Spanish ... 9

2. THE THREE MAJOR HISPANIC GROUPS 14

    2.1   Who are the Hispanics? – a brief introduction 16

        2.1.1.   The Chicano group 16

        2.1.2.   Historical background 20

        2.1.3.   Place names 22

        2.1.4.   Pachucho 23

        2.1.5.   Phonological characteristics of Chicano Spanish 23

        2.1.6.   Syntactic differences 25

        2.1.7.   Morphology 25

        2.1.8.   Lexical differences 25

        2.1.9.   Blackmar's division 26

        2.1.10.   The description of Chicanos by Moraga and Rodriguez 27

        2.1.11.   A critique of Chicano Spanish dialects and education 28

    2.2   Puerto Ricans 30

        2.2.1.   The history of the Puerto Ricans 30

    2.2.2. Bilingualism among Puerto Ricans 32

    2.2.3. Who are they? 35

    2.2.4. Mexicans and Puerto Ricans – comparision 36

  2.3 Cuban Spanish 36

3. OTHER SPANISH-SPEAKING GROUPS IN THE UNITED STATES 38

  3.1 Judeo-Spanish (Dzhudezmo) 38

  3.2 Louisansa Spanish: isleňo 39

    3.2.1. Spanish loanwords in English by 1900 40

    3.2.2. A chronological survey 42

4. PRESENT-DAY SPANISH IN AMERICAN ENGLISH 46

  4.1 Recent borrowings from Spanish into English (Garland Cannon) .. 46

    4.1.1. Background 46

    4.1.2. Semantic categories of Spanish 47

    4.1.3. Vocabulary 48

    4.1.4. The language of La Raza 48

    4.1.5. Grammar 49

    4.1.6. Phonology 49

    4.1.7. Productivity 50

    4.1.8. Well-known newly borrowed Spanish terms 50

  4.2 Ethnic nicknames of Spanish origin in American English 50

  4.3 Spanish place names in the United States 54

    4.3.1. Background 55

    4.3.2. Directions of borrowing 57

    4.3.3. Code-switching, code shifting 58

    4.3.4. Southwest-vocabulary in major English dictionaries 59

    4.3.5. Some well-known items from the lexicon of the Southwest 59

5. SPANISH TERMS IN AMERICAN LITERATURE 60

  5.1 Introduction 60

  5.2 William Sidney Porter (introduction) 61

  5.3 O. Henry's poetry 61

  5.4 Summary 65

6. SECOND LANGUAGE ACQUISITION, ERROR ANALYSIS 65

  6.1 Introduction 65

  6.2 Error analysis 65

    6.2.1. Translation 66

    6.2.2. Grammatically Judgement task 66

    6.2.3. Fill-in the blank 67

    6.2.4. Subjects 67

  6.3 Results 67

    6.3.1. Lexical items 68

6.3.2.	The neuter strategy: the COMP structure	69
6.3.3.	Empty COMP	70
6.3.4.	Language specific constructions	70
	6.3.4.1 Preposition stranding	70
	6.3.4.2 Nounless constructions	71
	6.3.4.3 Preposition copy	72
	6.3.4.4 Resumptive noun strategy	72
7.	**CONCLUSION**	**74**

HISTORICAL BACKGROUND

From the very beginning of its history, the United States have been a multiethnic and multicultural country. Nowadays there are two cultural forces standing against each other: the Anglo-Saxons and those derived from the immigrants, which are very slowly joining the mainstream of the predominant culture.

Today the number of people living in the United States is increasing. Most of the people coming to the United States arrived from countries where Spanish is the native language. After the African Americans they are the second largest minority group in the country. This group does not only represent the most significant linguistic minority group of the United States, but it is also the one that represents the highest rate of increase. The reason for this growth is first of all the continuous inflow of the Hispanic group from all over Latin America and a very high rate of birth. It is supposed that this growth results in one sixth of the United States population being Hispanic in the first decades of the twenty-first century (approximately 50 million people). Some scientists predict that in the future we can see the Hispanization of the country or the establishment of a completely parallel nation, while others see an assimilation or absorption of Hispanics. It appears that assimilation is continuously giving way to acculturation, and ethnic groups are increasingly adhering to their own values and characteristics to the point that the old idea of the "melting pot" is no longer valid.

1.1 Statistics

From these facts it is evident that the Spanish language is spoken natively by a large and diversified population in the United States. It is very difficult to determine their exact size, however, it is readily accepted that it is the largest "alloglotic" minority group of the country. For exact data we can rely only on imperfect census figures. According to the 1970 Census there are 9.6 million people of Spanish language, 9.3 million with Spanish heritage, or 9.1 million who are of Spanish origin. Presently, there are around ten million Hispanic people who live on the territory of the United States.

(Tescher, 1990:20)

1.2 The role of the Spanish language in daily life

According to a recent report's estimation, Spanish in the United States has a much more significant role than French. The Spanish language in the United States is studied nowadays by more than six million students and it is chosen as a second language by the majority of secondary school students (57,8 %), while French is studied by a much smaller rate (28%). The situation was different two generations before when the percentage of students studying these two languages was equal.

The high rate of increase of the Hispanic population, coupled with the great interest in Spanish, can be partly explained with the great wave of publications in Spanish. According to the *Asociación Nacional de Publicaciones Hispanas* (National Association of Hispanic Publications), more than 350 journals and magazines in the country did their publications in Spanish, that is 65 % more than in 1985. Taking only California into consideration, forty-five weeklies have come on the market in the last few years. Recently, in some nationally distributed newspapers, for instance in *The Washington Post,* there is a section in Spanish. Furthermore, there is an extensive Spanish International Network (SIN) that provides service for more than 300 television markets.

This interest in the Spanish language in the United States derives not exclusively from the linguistic but from the political and economic potential of the Hispanic sector, too. If Spanish is fashionable, it is first of all due to the fact that it is spoken by around 330 million people, and is the official language of all the countries in Central and South America except for Brasilia where the official language is Portuguese. Secondly, it is an official language of many significant international organisations such as the United Nations, UNESCO, and the European Union.

The increasing importance of the Spanish language in the United States is reflected in a large growth in research into the language over the last two decades, with a considerable body of work being produced for specialized journals, symposia and conferences, and published in several anthologies like Hernández Chávez et al. (1975), Bowen and Ornstein (1976), Amastae-Elias-Olivares (1982), Elías-Olivares (1983), Barkin et al. (1983), Gómez-Becker (1983), Aguirre (1984), Wherritt-García (1989), and Coulmas (1990). In a society which is fully aware of the sociolinguistic problems of bilingual education, most studies deal with the distinctive characteristic features of Spanish as it is spoken in the United States, and the alternations ("code switching") and inferences which are produced between the two languages. Since English is the dominant language, a lot of attention is paid to the influence of Spanish, especially when we consider those dialectal territories where the two languages combine with each other ("Spanglish"). However, less attention has been paid to the lexical borrowings brought into the English vocabulary owing to the contact with the Spanish language and culture.

It can be historically explained that the great majority of the Spanish loanwords in English have originated in the United States. Most of them are in general use, but a lot of them are peculiarities of American English, constituting one of its most distinctive characteristic features when compared with the British or other dialects of English.

English and Spanish nowadays are good instances of languages that incorporate loanwords with great ease. From the fact that Spanish has so many English loanwords, we can draw the conclusion that Spanish has had a cultural and ideological connection with the English language since the second world war. This attitude is in a sharp contrast with the characteristics of other languages such as the Hebrew of Israel or Icelandic, which until recent time have not borrowed words from other languages; that is to say they tried to preserve their ethnic identity. In this regard, English is not exempt from external influence. According to estimations, it is the language with the largest lexical inventory in the whole world. Since English has a high borrowing capacity, it has been typologically classified as a "heterogeneous language", while Romance languages such as Spanish are regarded as "amalgamate" because their parent language, Latin, is the main model for the formation of their learned vocabulary.

1.3 Historical, cultural issues

We can explain the composite structure of English partially by historical and cultural factors. From the very beginning, English has been in connection with the languages of different peoples in Europe like Celts, Teutons, Romans, Franks, etc., and as a consequence of the loss of declensions its linguistic system became more analytic and more open to borrowings. During the Renaissance, under new social conditions, the English vocabulary became richer; incorporated more that 100000 words, particularly taken from foreign sources, especially from the Romance and classical languages. The Spanish influence could be first felt in the sixteenth century, as a result of the cultural exchanges between Spain and England; this was when Spain was the predominant world power and Spanish military power was a great help to the emerging British empire. American English has continued this tradition of hospitality. Spanish influences American English to a great extent, which first of all can be accounted for the Spanish colonisation of America and later for the military interventionalism. Moreover, the third important factor is that the United States took away a great territory from Mexico, which now belongs to the southern part of the United States. Then came the conversion of the United States into a great world power, at the same time Britain politically and military became weaker and isolated. From that time the American way of life attracted a lot of people from all parts of the world who have left for the United States in the hope of greater prosperity, welfare and liberty.

After the Civil war a lot of Scandinavians, Slavs and Italians crossed the Atlantic Ocean. This wave of European immigrants was prolonged and it increased in the second quarter of the twentieth century when untold millions fled from the tyranny. Meanwhile, Spanish-speaking Mexicans and Puerto Ricans continued to flow in from the South. The influence of the foreign elements has become especially apparent in the general smoothing and down-toning of dynamic stress. The schwa cannot be heard at all in Spanish, Italian and these languages are spoken with clear and distinct demarcation of syllables. As a consequence, American speech has become like Spanish and Italian predominantly "staccato" and "marcato" while British English remains as such as Polish or Russian "legato" and "glissando": (Porter, 1969: 26)

> "In a way, American speech is more monotonous than British, but its meanings are far more easily assimilable. It makes fewer demands upon the hearer's attention and it is less assertive, less aggressive. Many Americans speak with small variety of tone, their tempo being slow"
>
> (Porter, 1990: 26)

The troublesome border that exists between Mexico and the United States is similar to the line, which is drawn between races and ethnicities within the latter country, particularly between whites on the one side and blacks and Indians on the other.

1.4 Anglicism – influence of English on the South American Spanish

French words used to have a significant influence on the Spanish language during the nineteenth century and at the beginning of the twentieth century; while nowadays, English words have this important role over Spanish.

> "The Anglicism have fully won the territory that was lost by Galicism. English has much more influence on Spanish spoken and written in our time than the French language".
>
> (Moreno de Alba, 1982: 50)

The presence of Anglicism is practically general in every dialect of Spanish, which may have several reasons and explanations but mainly the economic imperialism of the United States. If we need more accurate statements or data, we can refer to the news agencies and its influence on the press of the Spanish language, the predominance owned by this country in the boundaries of politics, industry, commerce, science, movies, sports and international relations. All of these facts have made the English language distinguished among other languages. Obviously, English words have come into not only the vocabulary of Spanish but to that of the majority of other languages to a great extent, too. The biography concerning Anglicism is abundant, but strictly from a dialectical point of view. There are few studies which include more or less extensive areas; the majority of investigations and calculations have reference to phenomena limited to a certain geographic zone or population. There are also suggestions how to classify the original English words into classes. Alvaro suggested a kind of classification that is to be taken into consideration:

1.) vulgar barbarisms: *guachiman, parquear*
2.) pochismos: characteristics of Spanish spoken in California and Texas which arose from anglicizing Spanish sounds and words: *marqueta-mercado* (market), *chopear-ir de compras* (do the shopping)
3.) Anglicisms: *crucial, ancestor, salvaguardar*
4.) The same Spanish forms but with difference in meaning for example the meaning of the English *apology* is "excuse" while its Spanish equivalent *apología* is used in the sense of "pleading"
5.) Spanish words with newly formed meanings: *aplicación* (solicitúd), *librería* (biblioteca)
6.) pure expressions, words in Anglo trends: *extender cortesías* (extend courtesy), *operar un negocio* (keep negotiation)
7.) solecisms that occur in Castilian sounds with English syntax: *estar siendo, cien por cien, acción a tomar*
8.) pure foreign phrases: *cake, film, snob*
9.) neologisms of unequivocal English influence: *boicotear, mecanizar*
10.) Anglo-Galicisms: *masacre, debut*

Alvaro's job has obviously more didactical than dialectological aim. It can be seen that for example there are certain requisites the author thinks that Anglicisms have to own in order to be able to be acceptable in the vocabulary of the Spanish language:

a.) lack of equivalent lexis in Spanish

b.) its use in respectable speakers

c.) should fit Spanish morphology

With regard to American Spanish, *Jeronimo Mallo* stated that in contrast to Galicisms which have a prevailingly literary presence (it should be taken into consideration that only the intellectuals read French books) Anglicisms are used by every Hispanic speaker in the fields of trade, politics, culture etc., especially owing to the fact that there is a developing intercommunication between the United States and Hispanic America. Some Anglicisms noted down by Mallo as characteristics of American scope are as follows:

- *estoy escribiendo (por escribo)* – I am writing
- *agradecerle (darle las gracias)* – to be grateful to someone
- *orden (pedido)* - order
- *viajar por avión (viajar en avión)* – travel by air
- *agenda (programa)* - programme
- *futuro (porvenir)* - future
- *apología (excusa)* - apology
- *aparente (cierto)* - apparent
- *audencía (auditorio)* - audience
- *barraca (quarte)* - cabin
- *tropas (soldados)* - soldiers
- *convención (reunión)* - convention
- *chanza (oportunidad)* - chance

- ***asistente (ayudante)*** - assistant
- ***romance (enamoriento)*** - romance
- ***argumento (discusión)*** - argument
- ***aplicación (solicitúd)*** - application
- ***congratulación (felicitación)*** - congratulation
- ***honesto (honrado)*** - honest

It is worth thinking of an affirmation that is not exclusive of Mallo, but it returns in every study about this subject. It is referred to the fact that the level of penetration of Anglicism in certain countries and regions is higher than in others.

> *"The diffusion of Anglicisms can be especially understood in Hispanic countries that have significant relationship with the United States, Puerto Rico, Mexico and Panama for geographic or any other reasons but it is necessary to underline the importance of working with studies of dialectological as well as comparable character in order to be able to decide which region shows stronger influence of Anglicisms"*

(Mello, 1990: 25)

This type of study does not exist for every country as it shows in a suitable way for Puerto Rico, Humberto López Morales (1982):

> *"The reexamination of bibliography demonstrates the absence of solid investigations, rigorously planned and performed which permits to make an undeniable conclusion in one or other sense. In Puerto Rican Spanish there is an overload of Anglicisms in contrast with no more than in other zones."*

(López, 1982: 20)

A systematic investigation for example can be that of Lope Blanch about Mexican Spanish extensively and strictly from a dialectical point of view. Among the thousands of words which can be maintained for a questionnaire of 4452 questions (each of which generally relied upon various lexical answers) could have hardly more than seventy Anglicism, which can be generally classified. It is to be taken into consideration that many of these words do not probably exist in the speech of other sociocultural levels (the popular for instance), which were not important in this investigation. Similarly, one must not forget that more than the third of Anglicisms, which are registered, belong to the semantic area of sports, many of which are practically indispensable. All these make us suppose that at least with these data we cannot provide that this geographic area has an estimable abundance of Anglicist lexis. In other equally systematic investigation in relation with Spanish in Havana, Humberto López Morales with the same questionnaire as Lope Blanch obtained a very low percentage (1.42 percent) for the Anglicisms. Sports seem to be the most affected field again. If some results were compared to the others, it could be determined perhaps whether in reality there are any countries the speakers of which use a greater number of Anglicist lexis. En Marius Sala, as stated above, the lexical material of many dictionaries and vocabularies of Americanisms and regionalisms are recommended in a nicely arranged way. From the point of view of geographic diffusion, the English words that are collected here, can be classified in the following ways:

a.) words at least spoken in five countries

b.) words spoken at least in three or four countries

c.) words spoken in only one or two countries

"The great majority of words which make up the first category are panamericans."
(José G. Moreno de Alba 1982: 43)

No less than 360 words belong to the first category. It seems to me interesting to show that more than three quarters of about 280 words of this list are not used either known in the communal Spanish of Mexico City. Taking into consideration not only the demographic difference of this human settlement (almost twenty million in the whole valley of Mexico) but first of all the fact that Mexico is generally mentioned as a country of overload of Anglicisms. If the (Anglicists) Mexican speakers only make use of one such a low percentage of words and phrases described like panamerican, it will be clear that the dictionaries and vocabularies of Americanisms do not only prove to be little reliable when speaking about Indian words and phrases as Morigo confirmed but regional lexicons also seem to try to incorporate as many Anglicisms as possible no matter if they are used or not.

Later the same investigators made a list about not panamerican Anglicisms and demonstrated that "analyzing the inventory we observed that these expressions can be found in the geographic zones of evident English influence: Central America, the Antilles, the Caribbean, Mexico and the Hispanic speaking-region of the United States". It must be shown again that in Mexico only thirteen expressions out of fifty on the list are known:

cornflakes, curricular, jonrón, mofle/niple, panti, porcharse (being lazy), rin, rompope, sóquet, teoretico, trailer, zíper

In conclusion, on the one hand the result is that practically it is impossible to find examples for Anglicisms in the countries of Latin America, and do not belong to the so-called internationals. On the other hand, we cannot trust the fact that we are able to determine the frequency of the use of words of English origin only with the help of dictionaries and with the investigation of words spoken in certain regions.

2. THE THREE MAJOR HISPANIC GROUPS

The United States is a country of many cultures, which through immigrants had an influence on the American way of life today. Some of these immigrants who had a profound effect were the Hispanics – that is people who are from Spanish-speaking countries such as Mexico, Puerto Rico, Santo Domingo and Cuba. In 1950 the population of the United States included fewer than four million Spanish speakers. By the mid 1980s this number had increased to sixteen or seventeen million and is still rising quickly. Consequently, in some parts of the country, especially in the Southwest, South and Southern California it is more common to hear Spanish than English.

The Cuban Americans, whose number is 500000, settled down first of all in New York City (New Jersey) and Florida. The second largest Spanish American group came from Puerto Rico (1.5 million), most of those people who accumulated in the ghettoes of New York City. The most numerous group came originally from Mexico and constitutes sixty percent of the Hispanic population (five million) in the United States. Their process of immigration is still going on, which is primarily due to economic reasons. They settled down primarily in the southwestern part of the

United States, in states like Texas, Arizona, Colorado, New Mexico and California. This group speaks the Chicano variety of English, which is the most uniformed variety among the Spanish American varieties of English expressing ethnic solidarity for a large number of people. Immigrants from Cuba and Puerto Rico represent relatively recent immigration, but about eighty percent of the Cuban population is foreign-born. The Mexican Americans, however, represent much greater heterogeneity and diversity ranging from 750000 immigrants being born in Mexico to the interdeterminable number who trace their ancestral settlement in New Mexico back to as early as Juan de Oñate's colonization party of 1598.

(Richard V. Teshner, 1990: 30)

These are the three major Hispanic groups but beside them there are also the *Isleño Spanish* speakers of Louisana, who are descendants of early colonists from the Canary Islands, the speakers of *Dzhudezmo* or in other words *Judeo-Spanish*, who have immigrated to the United States mainly in recent years, and communities of other groups who immigrated from Spain, Central and South America and even the Philippines.

The reason why they came to the United States was the same as those of earlier immigrants from Europe, to escape from poverty and political persecution in their homeland.

2.1 Who are the Hispanics? – a brief introduction

In 1985 the government estimated that there were millions of illegal immigrants in the United States, the majority of whom had arrived from Mexico, crossing the Rio Grande, the frontier between Mexico and the United States. In the United States the term *Spanish people* is used to refer without discrimination to any person that speaks Spanish. This definition is imprecise in the sense that it includes people from more than two dozen countries, all of whom originate from the American continent, the Caribbean and Spain. To use this term for all Spanish speakers is not generally accepted as it would be also incorrect to regard all citizens as English in New-Zealand, Australia or United States.

The term *Latino* refers to people who originate or have a heritage related to Latin America in recognition of the fact that this group of people actually is a mixture of many nationalities. Since the term *Latin* comes into use as the least common name for all peoples of Latin America in recognition of the fact that some Romance languages such as Spanish, Portuguese, French are the native tongue of the majority of Latin Americans, this term is widely acceptable by most of the people. However, it is not appropriate to use this term for the millions of native Americans who inhabit the territory.

By the term *Hispanics* we usually mean all Spanish speakers. However, more accurately by this name we mean a descent or cultural heritage related to Spain. Since many millions of people who speak Spanish are not of real Spanish origin (e.g. native Americans) and millions more who live in Latin America but do not speak Spanish or have Spanish heritage (e.g. Brazilians), it is not correct to use this term as a collective name for all Spanish speakers and may actually be cause for offensive.

2.1.1. The Chicano group

As it has been stated above, this group represents the largest, most numerous people among the Hispanics in the United States. Though the present Chicano population is primarily the result of the immigration of Mexican nationals in the past 125 years or so that the Southwest has become a part of the United States, it is important to concentrate on the fact that the ancestors of an important number of this group had settled in the Southwest long before it became part of the United States and, indeed, long before there existed a United States or Mexico. Due to the fact that they have a four hundred-year history of fluctuating but continuous immigration, the group itself is very heterogeneous. From a sociological point of view, it may still refuse unitary classification, but from a linguistic aspect we must look at it as a unit. At this point it is necessary to explain why this offensive label "Chicano" was chosen to refer to the group and language variety alike. We can use a lot of terms: Mexican, Chicano, Latin American, Latin, Mexican American, Spanish American, Spanish, Hispano, Spanish-surnamed, and others; these are used for ethnic identification by different segments of the group and by outsiders, as well. However, if the term is acceptable for one group, for the other it may be offensive. The label *Mexican,* which is selected by Cárdenas could be related to the groups who are characterized by ancestral residence within Mexico's borders. By this term, we mean the nationality of all people who inhabit the territory of Mexico. Therefore, this is applied appropriately for Mexican citizens who are visitors or workers in the United States (They were born in the United States or are naturalized citizens of the United States who are of Mexican origin). These people feel it important to make a distinction. Citizens of the United States who are troubled by this often emphasize that most immigrants do not distinguish themselves by their exact origin (i.e.: German American) but simply refer to themselves as *Americans*. The term *Mexican Spanish* is not precise enough to distinguish it from the Spanish of Mexico, consequently, the term *Mexican-American* is often employed. *Chicano,* on the other hand, has the general meaning of Mexican (these two forms derive from the same source) whereas referring to the distinctively *American* variant, too. Now it seems that the term *Chicano* is appropriate not only because it is increasingly accepted by different members of the group, but also because it is related to the unity of the linguistically unified group that we would like to label. *Chicano* is a relatively recent term that many Mexican descendants regard as very specific and therefore this label reflects their unique culture though its first usage seems to have been discriminatory. The most likely source of the word is traced to the 1930 and 40s period when as a result of the agreement between the governments of Mexico and the United States, rural Mexicans, often native Americans were imported to the United States to provide cheap field labor. The expression came into use in the fields of California in a negative sense first: the Nauhatl speakers were considered to be ridiculous because they were unable to pronounce the term *Mexicanos* in the right way. They regarded themselves as *Mexicanos* but pronounced the term according to the rules of pronunciation of their language: *Mesheecanos*. That is the reason why they were mocked very often. Whatever its source may be, it was at first offensive to be identified by this name. The expression was appropriated by Mexican-American activists who participated in the Brown Power movement of the sixties and seventies in the United States Southwest, and has now become accepted and is widely used. Since this expression is preferred by political activists and by those people whose main purpose is to establish a new identity for their culture, it still has an unpleasant connotation for more assimilated Americans.

Definitely, Chicano Spanish is the best described among the Spanish varieties in the United States. This is due no doubt to the size of the group, its heterogeneity, and the depth of its roots on the territory. However, the length of the roots can apparently often be seen to be in correlation to a large extent with the volume of research. Owing to this fact, it will be very useful to survey the situation according to geographical boundaries: New Mexico and Southern Colorado, Arizona, Texas, California, northern Colorado, the Midwest, the Northwest, etc.

About 150 years ago, the United States took illegaly half of the territory of what was then Mexico as spoils of war and in a series of land 'sales' that were forced into capitalizing on the United States triumph in that war and on Mexico's weak political and economic situation. As a result, a significant number of Mexican citizens was acknowledged to be citizens of the United States very rapidly, and the treaty which declared peace between the two countries "recognized the rights of such people to their private properties, their own religion (Roman Catholicism) and the right to speak and receive education in their own native language (for the majority Spanish)".

(Porter, 1969: 45)

Therefore, the descendants of this population continue to fight for such rights, and many hold that theirs is a colonised land and people in view of the fact that their territory and population were taken over by military force. Another and more numerous group of the United States citizens of Mexican origin are either descendants of, or are themselves, people who regard themselves as temporarily placed from Mexico by economic circumstances. As opposed to the waves of European immigrants who willingly went away from their homelands as a consequence of class and religious discrimination, and whose aim was to make their lives anew in the "New World" and never to return to the "old land", these displaced Mexicans typically preserve strong family connections in Mexico and usually intend to return to Mexico provided they can become economically secure and richer. Therefore, these people bring up their children according to their norms; in such a way to get them accustomed to their own language, religion and cultural habits.

However, there is a great tension within this population: between those of Mexican birth who perceive themselves as temporary guests in the United States and their descendants who are born in the United States, are acculturated with the norms, customs of United States society in public school and are not motivated by the same connections that bind a migrant generation of Mexicans. This establishes a classic "niche" of descendants of immigrants who are full-fledged United States citizens, but who typically cannot have all the rights and privilidges of citizenship because they maintain strong cultural identity deriving from their upbringing and education. This group of people feels that it is really necessary to distinguish themselves from both its United States environment and its "Mexican Mother Culture", which does not typically welcome or accept "extravagants". This is definitely a unique set of people, in the respect that this group has both strong connections and strong discrimination from United States and Mexican mainstream parent cultures. As a result, they established a completely new culture of their own which needs its own name and identity.

There is no single name for these seven million Americans of Mexican descent. In California they are often referred to as Mexican Americans or "mexicanos" while in Texas they are regarded as Latin Americans or "tejanos". In New Mexico the descendants of colonists who arrived in the 1600s and 1700s prefer to call themselves "nuevo mexicanos" or "Hispanos". Nowadays many of the younger members of the group, and especially activists tend to use the term "Chicano". This expression, a form of "mexicano" was made shorter by dropping the first syllable, had a somewhat pejorative connotation at the beginning of this century, but many young Americans of Mexican origin have been using it as a symbol of pride since the second world war.

2.1.2. *Historical background*

The history of the Mexican Americans can be conveniently divided into five broad time periods: the Indo-Hispanic period, the Mexican period, a period of cultural conflict during the last half of the nineteenth century, a period of resurgence in the first four decades of the twentieth century, and a period of regeneration from World War I to the present time.

The first period includes the development of Indian civilizations in Mexico, their defeat by Spanish conquerors, the beginning of *mestizaje,* the blending of Indian and Spanish cultures, colonisation of the present-day Southwest of the United States from Central Mexico, and finally, the movement of independence from Spain at the beginning of the nineteenth century.

The "grito de dolores" (scream of pains) can be considered to be the beginning of the Mexican era in 1810, and political events bring into focus the gulf that existed between the Mexican heartland and the northern frontier. By this period cultures, which are different to some extent from each other but are basically related to the mother culture had developed, and continuing isolation led to mounting political differences and unrest. The end of this period was a battle with the United States, which was finished as a result of the Treaty of Guadalupe Hidalgo. According to the treaty Mexico lost fifty percent of its original territory which was ceded to the United States.

From 1848 to the end of the nineteenth century, the third time period can be characterized by the influences of Anglo-American migration towards the Southwest; investment of capital in mines, railroads, cattle, and agriculture.

The main characteristics of the fourth period was that more and more people migrated to the United States through the Mexican border. In this migratory movement Mexican Americans settled down not only in the traditional Southwest but also in the agricultural and industrial centers of Midwest and North. This era witnessed also the development of Mexican American organizational efforts and a reserved migratory trend of forced repatration during the depressed thirties.

With the beginning of the second world war we can see the contemporary period when migration goes on to the United States; this process is regarded as a revival of self-awareness and recognition of the cultural values of the Mexican heritage particularly among Chicano youths; there is some development in social conditions of *la raza;* and powerful movements for having a greater role in the American way of life through the insistence of education, full civil rights, and equality of economic opportunity.

From a historical point of view, there have been two Anglo-American views of the Mexican American, both inaccurate. One ignored his Indian background and regarded him as a Spanish *hidalgo* (aristocrat), the descendant of the great conquerors. The other concept was more widespread which derived from the American frontier experience. This second Anglo-American wave did not take into consideration the Spanish heritage and saw the Mexicans as Indians who are characterized as lazy, dirty and given to drinking and thievery. The Mexican American is often inaccurately stereotyped as an agricultural worker who is a dweller in a rural area or in a small town. Although it is true that Mexican Americans constitute a significant part of the farm labor force in the Southwest, today the overwhelming majority of them are urbans. As time passed, more and more Mexican Americans moved to bigger settlements, by the 1970s more than eighty percent of Mexican Americans lived in cities.

The concept of many otsiders that the majority of native-born Mexican Americans cannot speak English is not true. Most of them prefer to speak Spanish in certain situations, and many native-born children have been brought up in homes where Spanish is spoken. However, Mexican Americans are different from other groups (for example from German Americans) in the sense that they did not establish their own education system and most of them go only to public schools.

The historical past of Mexican Americans has established at least three subcultures, namely those of "californio", "tejano", and "nuevo mexicano". The three groups have been influenced in different ways by their economic and social backgrounds in Mexico, their dates of settlement in the Southwest, the geography and natural resources of the settlement area, their degree of interaction with local Indians, and the volume of recent immigration from Mexico. Only in California, there are nowadays at least six groups: descendants of early "californio" families, those who immigrated there during World War I and the 1920s, *braceros* (day laborer) who arrived there during the period of World War II, those of "nuevo mexicanos" (who consider themselves more Spanish than Mexican), those of "tejanos" who have left for the States, and those persons of Mexican origin whose assimilation into the general California community has been so pronounced that they have lost all sense of being part of *la raza* (the race).

In spite of these differences, Mexican Americans constitute a basic cultural unity who preserved their ethnic traits, customs and traditions. Some of these are the Spanish language, pride in their cultural and historical heritage, preference for native arts, crafts and foods. Since World War II, the expansion of Spanish-language radio and television programs have reinforced these cultural elements. These days the unity between the members of the Chicano community is due to the establishment of a great number of political and ethnic organizations.

Generally speaking, Mexican Americans had their own specific values, which are different from those of Anglo-Saxon society. Mexican Americans have a strong connection towards their family and kinship, furthermore, they concentrate on such values as individual worth which is based on honor, respect and machismo (virile manliness). Their opinion is that the individual value of one person is much more important than his success and achievements.

2.1.3. Place names

The Spanish and Mexican settlers gave name to their surroundings, which reflect their customs, tradition and culture. Some of the place names come from a description of their territory, the meaning of *'Buena Vista'* for example is that of beautiful view. Other places were named in honour of a particular saint or because these were discovered on that Saint's day (San Francisco, San Diego, San Antonio). The state *Florida* received its name when it was discovered on *el Dia de las flores pascuas* (Eastern Sunday). Still others got their name after famous persons like *Ponce de Leon* or *Hidalgo*. Some inhabitants named their surroundings deriving from a religious idea such as *Trinidad* which means Trinity. Lastly, there are some Spanish or Mexican place names in the country, which are the same as in Spain like *Granada* or as in Mexico like *Zapata*.

2.1.4. Pachucho

The term *Pachucho*, the Southwest Spanish argot that is nationally popular in connection with gangs of Chicano deliquents during the 1940s, is referred to by several other names like *caló, tirilí,* etc. Like other argots, Pachucho deviates from general Chicano Spanish primarily concerning its lexicon, which derives from several sources. First of all, the studies of Pachucho concentrate on the collection of non-standard vocabulary items and on their etymological explanation. One major report is that of Barker's separate publication on *Tucson Pachucho* (1950), which is famous for its analysis of usage and attitudes as for its vocabulary list. A more thorough documentation of the connections between *Pachucho* and other contemporary Hispanic argots is provided by A. Trejo's excellent collection of Latin American argot forms (1968).

2.1.5. Phonological characteristics of Chicano Spanish

1.) In Chicano English voiced ending consonants for example /z/ are pronounced generally without voicing. Consequently, *please* is pronounced similarly as the word *police,* in the case of *easy,* they pronounce /isɪ/ instead of /izɪ/. The voiced /d/ will become /t/; for example they pronounce the word *'hid'* with a voiceless consonant like /hɪt /.

2.) The labiodental /v/ will be a bilabial /b/.

3.) The sounds in American English such as /Θ/ and /ð/ are pronounced in Chicano dialect in a different way: Chicano English speakers tend to say /t/ instead of /Θ/ and /d/ instead of /ð/. This case occurs only in initial position, when a particular word begins with one of these sounds.

4.) Another very important characteristic feautre of Chicano English is word ending consonant simplification. This means that word ending consonants are omitted. From this fact it can be seen that there is no difference between the pronunciation of the two words like *star* and *start*. Moreover, a grammatical morpheme can be omitted too like in the word *towed* /to/ instead of /tod/, /s/ designating third person singular drops out for instance from the word *loves* which then will be pronounced as /lav/.

5.) Speakers of Chicano English mix /tʃ/ and /ʃ/ in their pronunciation. A normal English speaker says the word *check* with the pronunciation of /tʃek/ while in Chicano speech we can hear /ʃek/. Furthermore, it is interesting to observe how they pronounce the words *show* and *chicken:* /tʃoʊ/ and /ʃiken/.

6.) In standard American English there are eleven stressed vowel phonemes: /ɪ/, /i/, /e/, /ɛ/, /æ/, /u/, /ʊ/, /o/, /ɔ/, /ʌ/, /a/. In the Spanish language there are only five: /i/,/e/,/u/,/o/,/a/. Consequently, Chicano English speakers use these five sounds instead of the eleven English vowels, which means a bending of particular vowels. From this fact we can come to the conclusion that from the two sounds such as /ɪ/ and /i/ there will be an /i/ in Chicano English. The phonetic transcription of the two nouns such as *ship* and *sheep* will be the same: /ʃip/.

7.) Another very important difference can be seen in the way of stressing; in many cases stressing in Chicano English is not the same as in standard American English especially in the case of compound nouns. In the word *miniskirt* the main stress falls in standard American English to the beginning of the word (miniskirt), while in Chicano English it falls to the second syllable, like (mini'skirt); *an'ticipate* in Chicano English is pronounced as *antici'pate*.

Another significant characteristic feature is related to that of intonation. In Chicano English a declarative sentence is pronounced with rising intonation while in standard American English such kind of sentence like this is characterized by falling intonation.

2.1.6. Syntactic differences

1.) The result of the influence of Spanish on English is that in Chicano English we can find double negation in sentences:

Standard American English	Chicano English
I do not have any money.	*I do not have no money.*
I do not want anything.	*I do not want nothing.*

2.) The other remarkable difference concerns adjectives; in Chicano English the comparative form *'more'* is used in the sense of *'more often'*.

Standard American English	Chicano English
I use English more often.	*More I use English.*
They use Spanish more often.	*They use more Spanish.*

2.1.7. Morphology

Differences concerning morphology are noteworthy considering uncountable nouns in standard English whereas in Chicano English these nouns are regarded as countable. Those who speak Chicano English say *"vacations"* instead of *"vacation"* or *"an applause"* instead of *"applause"*.

2.1.8. Lexical differences

In this variety there are certain lexical special characteristics, which are related to the meaning of words. The word *borrow* in Chicano English stands for *lend*. One who speaks standard American English asks like this: "*Lend me a pencil!*" The case in Chicano speech is different: "*Borrow me a pencil!*"

Another example is the adverb *until* which in Chicano English means negation. If the response for the question like "*Is X here?*" is "*Until three*", in Chicano speech it means that "*X is not here until three*".

Concerning vocabulary, Chicano English is influenced by Spanish to a great extent, too. Chicano speakers very often use the term *quinceanera* which for them means a party for the teenager girls of fifteen. Other examples which are worth mentioning are *compadre (*godfather), *comadre (*godmother).

The majority of Chicano English speakers are bilinguals; that is to say that they speak both varieties: Chicano English and standard American English.

2.1.9. Blackmar's division

Blackmar's primary purpose was to examine how language is used in the Southwest. He found that the Southwest consists of two varieties of the Spanish language. The first is called

> *"the old Castilian language, which is still spoken by few remaining aristocratic families of two blood."*
>
> (Blackmar, 1996:30)

This dialect is a bit different from modern continental Spanish, as compared with other modern languages, it changes very little as the time goes on. The second dialect is refered to as "Mexican"; it is quite extensively used in New Mexico and California by the great majority of the people of Spanish blood and their native converts to Christianity, and is a source of great worry for Blackmar, because

> *"it is through the language of the common people, through the Spanish language clipped and degraded by the commingling of unlettered Spaniards with an inferior race, that words find their way into English."*
>
> (Blackmar, 1996: 30)

Blackmar very strongly opposes the use of those phrases which are used in the Southwest on a temporal basis such as *mucho frio* (very cold), *mucho caliente* (very hot), *poco tiempo* (little time), *muchas gracias* (many thanks), *si Señor* (yes man), etc. Their primary influence can be felt when the use of good English dispappears; fortunately this fact does lead him to the ignorance of Spanish words and expressions which are universally accepted like *adobe, cañon, tule, rodeo, loco, burro* etc.

2.1.10. The description of Chicanos by Moraga and Rodriguez

While Blackmar concentrated on the use of the language in the Southwest, these two people wrote a lot about the cultural background of the group. They were more interested in their past, culture than their race.

When people consider a particular person to be a Chicano, for Rodriguez that label does not suggest a cultural term but refers to a racial identity. He writes about bilingual education concerning primarily Hispanics whose native language is Spanish. He thinks that people should learn the language of the country, in this case English. If all Spanish speakers learn English, it is possible that many of them will go through what he went through, namely, a loss of culture. Probably, the loss of culture influences the race as a whole. In Rodriguez's essay race and culture are closely connected. If Hispanic is his race but Chicano is his culture, it seems as though these two went hand in hand.

Moraga faces a different framework than Rodriguez. People do not assume that she is a Chicano; people see her as a white, in her family, light skin was "right". Meaning that if she were able to pass as a white, she might not be treated badly. She was not taught Spanish at home, but she picked up some of the phrases that were insulting for lower income Mexicans. Her family wanted her to be able to "pass in the white world". Being white meant getting ahead in life and becoming succesful. She also felt that being educated enough might make people forget her background and people would not consider her to be of Chicana origin. Both Moraga and Rodriguez thought that education is a good way to go ahead which would help erase the fact that they were not white. They both tried to reject parts of their culture, their values and their roots. It seems that both of them may not, or at one point did not see themselves as Chicanos or Hispanics, but owing to their outside appearance and backgrounds, they could not betray society.

2.1.11. A critique of Chicano Spanish dialects and education

This critique stems from Ernest García 1971, whom Gonzáles takes to task for stating that the existence of such forms as *hablates, comites, vivites* results from the transfer of internal –s- from penultimate syllable-final to word final position. He argues convincingly that since in addition to these forms, Chicano Spanish also employs other variants that preserve -s- in penultimate syllable-final position (hablastes-*spoke* etc.), any analysis must take into consideration the subjection of the second person singular preterit to two possibilities:

- regularization, in which the final -s- is added such as all other second person singular forms
- deletion of the internal -s-. Consequently, for *hablastes* (spoke) only the first rule applies; for *hablates* both apply. In any event,

> *"the above analyses are not really new at all [since] Ramón Menéndez Pidal...cites evidence of existence of such forms in the early eighteenth century and proposed the same rules posited above."*

(González, 1996:42)

González does not agree with Garcia's treatment of such differences as the first-person plural marker of the verb (–mos>nos) when the stress falls on the antepenultimate syllable. He also makes a critique about the rearrangement of the infinitive of certain "radical changing" verbs to conform to the changed root, the "reduction" of *el* (male definite article*)* and *la* (female definite article) to */* before any word beginning with a vowel, etc.

Various intelligent comments concerning the issue of accepting Chicano Spanish dialects in schools follow the strictly linguistic discussions. The author suggests correcting such "baby talk" overgeneralizations as *sabo, ero* and *pongaba* on the grounds that

> *"our guide should be the language spoken by the adult Chicano community"*

(Gonzáles, 1996: 43)

for that reason, terms like *pidí, sigí* are accepted in the classroom, which does not mean though, that their standard alternates *pedí, segí* should be prohibited, since

> *"failure to learn (at least passively) other forms of the Spanish language will control the Chicano in his exchange of ideas with other people - particularly the writings of our ancestors. Or should we wait for the English translation?"*
>
> (Gonzáles, 1996:44)

González also opposes code-switching in the classroom on the grounds that its greatest danger

> *"would be the tendency for the pupils to revert to the stronger of their two languages instead of attempting new things in language being learned."*
>
> (Gonzáles, 1996:44)

2.2 Puerto Ricans

2.2.1. The history of the Puerto Ricans

The Puerto Rican group on the United States continent is a relatively recent phenomenon. It is true that a particular number of Puerto Ricans went to New York City even before World War II, but most of the recent population is the consequence of post-World War II immigration, the heaviest migration was during the late 1940s and throughout the 1950s. Very few Puerto Ricans came to the mainland until after WWII because of high cost and infrequency of transportation. It was only after the war's end when cheap transportation to the mainland started going on. As a consequence, Puerto Rican migration flourished. Furthermore, since this transportation was based in New York City, *barrios* (quarters) developed there first rather than in Florida which was closer to Puerto Rico. According to the estimation of the 1970 Census, more than ninety-five percent of the mainland Puerto Rican population reported the island as their own place of birth of a parent. New York City is the present home of the great majority of the Puerto Rican population – maybe as many as two-thirds out of the total.

Most Puerto Ricans who immigrated to the United States had to face two serious problems: poverty and race discrimination. The indigenous Amerindian population of the island was largely murdered by the Spanish conquerors and the diseases they brought with them. The Spanish introduced African slavery to the island in 1511 which was over in 1873 and there is a large mixture of white and black ancestry in the island's population. According to the point of view of social theorists like Myrdal, blacks and Puerto Ricans in New York City and elsewhere ought to be political allies but in reality they are more often rivals.

For Puerto Ricans the United States meant a land of opportunity. Their immigration to the country was a difficult process. They had to cope with discrimination problems in many walks of life in the United States. Finally, in the twentieth century they realized that they were able to stand up for their rights. The first migration began in the 1860s which was the period when the migration to the United States started to grow. The United States found it necessary to carry on a capitalistic way of life, which in turn brought about the problems of overpopulation. One way for the United States to cope with this dilemma was to ship many people from Puerto Rico to the United States. When they reached the mainland, they began to work for very low wages. Puerto Ricans had absolutely no word in what their salary should be. They only received 0.5 USD above the minimum wage for agricultural workers in New Jersey. They also had to face low wages when they went to Hawaii at the end of the nineteenth century where they were rivals with the immigrants from Japan. The Puerto Ricans were considered to be dirty and they were favoured by the Japanese. In this way, they were compelled to work for incredibly low wages.

During the period of 1898 to 1917 the Puerto Ricans who were living in the United States were considered to be citizens of nowhere. In 1901 according to the Supreme Court's decision Puerto Rico belonged to the United States territory, but Puerto Ricans could not be representatives of the country. The Americans thought that they could just claim this land to be their own but could not claim full responsibility for it. At that time Puerto Rico was inhabited by only one million people. By the year, 1917 Congress passed an act that made Puerto Ricans "citizens". Even though this act stated that Puerto Ricans were "citizens" of the United States, the Puerto Ricans still did not have a place that they would truly call home from a legal point of view. But because this law was made, it created a relationship between the mainland United States and the island Puerto Rico, which brought about the industrialization of Puerto Rico, and eventually the mass of migration to the United States.

During the 1960s the "class politics" struggle for Puerto Ricans in the United States turned into an issue of ethnic politics. Through this hard time during the sixties and seventies many groups turned up that fought for equal rights for minority groups. The Puerto Ricans created many of their own communities and through their hard times created a form of solidarity amongst themselves. Some of the groups that were formed were the Puerto Rican Political Action Committee (PRPAC), and the Young Lord's Party. Jose Cruz in his book, *Identity and Power* writes about these new issues that were based on ethnicity and the Puerto Ricans' struggle to find their own identity. Cruz believed that class politics had already been established by Puerto

Ricans. He also believed that Puerto Rican communities should place some people of their own ethnic background in government positions. He states that these officials should not do what the white man tells them, however, he listens to his people and stands up for their rights to make a difference. In the movie "*Palante*", we can see how difficult it was for the Puerto Ricans to be recognized as equal citizens of the United States.

The sixties was also a difficult time for them because they were sent to war to Vietnam, to fight for a country that could not even fully recognize them as citizens. The Vietnam War also forced many people to establish organizations that stood up for their rights. The Puerto Ricans moved to the mainland of the United States to make a better way of life for themselves than they had in Puerto Rico. Although at the beginning of the Puerto Rican wave of migration things seemed to be working out, but everything turned to the worse when jobs began disappearing and discrimination did not get any better. The organizations that were established in the sixties and seventies provided a greater help for the life of the Puerto Ricans in the United States. Puerto Ricans are now fully recognized as citizens of the United States. Although the struggle still exists, Puerto Ricans have come a long way and have many people in politics that represent a strong voice for many of the Puerto Rican communities. Cruz helped stand up for ethnic politics and gave the way for many of them soon to be Puerto Rican-American leaders.

2.2.2. *Bilingualism among Puerto Ricans*

For more than 400 years Puerto Rico was a colony of Spain. In 1890 the island came under the control of the United States. During the nineteenth century, Puerto Ricans received United States citizenship and could travel from mainland United States without restrictions. The island now has a population of only less than four million persons and almost three million Puerto Ricans inhabit the mainland United States.

During the Spanish domination, the principal language was Spanish. When the Americans assumed control, there were attempts to introduce the English language, but Spanish remained the official language. The recent political landscape in Puerto Rico is divided amongst those who want independence, statehood or commonwealth status. The supporters of this thought agreed that Spanish should be the language of Puerto Rico. Still the fact remains that a particular amount of official and commercial business in Puerto Rico is conducted in English. More importantly, most of the very large Puerto Rican communities who inhabit the mainland United States have certainly found themselves learning English, either out of necessity or circumstances.

According to a survey, results from the TGI Puerto Rico study, there were more than two thousand individuals aged more than twelve or older who were interviewed between February and April 1999. When they were asked the question which language they spoke, seventy-two percent answered that they spoke only Spanish, twelve percent said mostly Spanish, fifteen percent said both Spanish and English, while only one percent stated that they spoke mostly or only English.

The ability to speak English and Spanish is correlated with actual experience in mainland United States. The following table demonstrates the percentage of people who have travelled to somewhere in the United States during twelve months.

Total	Speak only Spanish	Speak mostly Spanish	Speak Spanish and English	Speak mostly or always English
13%	10%	18%	20%	17%

The demographic characteristics of bilingual people speaking both English and Spanish:

Gender	Age	Percentage
Male	12-17	7%
Male	18-24	16%
Male	25-34	16%
Male	35-49	17%
Male	50-64	16%

Male	65+	16%
Female	12-17	12%
Female	18-24	20%
Female	25-34	14%
Female	35-49	15%
Female	50-64	18%
Female	65+	15%

ANNUAL HOUSEHOLD INCOME	PERCENTAGE
9999 USD or less	10%
10000-14999 USD	13%
15000-19999 USD	20%
20000-24999 USD	33%
25000-29999 USD	36%
30000 USD or more	26%
TOTAL	15%

(website: *www.PuertoRicans.com*, 1998)

For the island Puerto Rico Spanish is unquestionably the principal language of daily use as well as the essence of their self-identity. But Puerto Ricans who have stayed in mainland United States may in fact speak more fluent English than Spanish. The fact that they became scattered and settled down in the United States gave way to the development of "Spanglish" (a mixture of English and Spanish). This has led to the matter of language competence and its relationship to economic welfare with the question of whether bilingualism among Puerto Ricans has hindered the development of linguistic, cognitive and educational skills in such a way that they are unable to study well in school and complete effectively at work.

2.2.3. Who are they?

The Census Bureau groups many Puerto Ricans into two main categories: they are both black and Puerto Ricans. Among the Hispanic groups, Puerto Ricans are at the bottom or near the bottom according to most of the criteria by which the disadvantaged are measured.

A lot of data demonstrate that the second and the third generation among the Puerto Ricans have tended to improve their economic and educational status. For the majority of the immigrant groups it was also true that those who moved away from the established center of immigration (for Puerto Ricans it was New York City) had usually higher incomes. This applied as well for the very few number of Puerto Ricans in San Francisco, Los Angeles and Lorain (Ohio). The latter group has demonstrated high social mobility: in the 1970s more than fifty percent of the families had their own homes, and women were the head of only seven percent of the Puerto Rican families there. A survey demonstrated that in 1980 the first two generations of Puerto Ricans were outside New York City, most of them were in the nearby states like Connecticut and Pennsylvania.

The religion of the Puerto Rican community is different from that of the native Americans, when they arrived in the United States, they felt alienated from the American church. However, Puerto Ricans do not have many priests who migrated with them, even on the island only about one-third of the Catholic clergy are ethnic Puerto Ricans. The United States Catholic Conference's purpose was to meet the demands of the Spanish-speaking communities in the way that they established bureaucratic organizations, which was not really effective for the Puerto Ricans though. As the demonstration shows, half of the Catholics in Manhattan and Brooklyn are Spanish speakers (Puerto Ricans are the largest of those), the hierarchy is, from top to bottom, dominated by European ethnics, especially by Irish Americans.

2.2.4. Mexicans and Puerto Ricans – comparision

Mexicans and Puerto Ricans have not only the language in common but they also share religion and poverty. On the other hand, they do not have any other special characteristics in common though. They live in different territories, they have different traditions and they are regarded as being of different races: the majority of Puerto Ricans are considered to be black while Mexicans are viewed as white, however, each group is more accurately described as having mixed racial origin. We can see a remarkable difference in the school dropout rate: in Puerto Rico American style school systems have been established for almost one hundred years. For example, one school system in New York City accepts not only Americans but other ethnic minorities as well. The picture in the Southwest is just the opposite: in California the purpose for many decades was to exclude Mexican Americans. The economic differences can be accounted for the fact that a great number of Mexican American population inhabits the so-called Sunbelt, which in recent years has been the most dynamic part of the United States economically. Puerto Ricans, on the other hand, are concentrated in a region where the development is not so dynamic and where there is no work opportunity for those who are unskilled.

2.3 Cuban Spanish

There have been certain enclaves of Cubans in the United States recently, but the great majority of the population have been immigrating to the United States since the 1959 Fidel Castro revolution. According to the 1970 Census estimation there are approximately eighty percent of the Cuban community in the United States who were born in Cuba. In 1898, when Cuban liberation from Spain was achieved partly due to American support and patronage during the period of Spanish-American war, Cuba gained independence. However, there was in fact an American protectorate for six decades, a protectorate which was over only by Fidel Castro's revolution in 1959. During that long period, Cuban Americans settled down continuously in the United States. As a consequence of the fact that people constantly came and went, the number of this population fluctuated in the country. The first Cuban American community was in Key West, Florida, where a Cuban-owned cigar factory provided the basis for a settlement of fifty people in 1831. First of all, cigar-making centers flourished in New York City (New Jersey), Tampa (Florida) which used Cuban tobacco and employed Cuban workers. Later on, New York City was overwhelmed by European people, but Tampa is characterized by Cuban dominance even in the present days. After the liberation of Cuba the immigration was very sparse for about half a century. In 1950 the Census found that there were thirty thousand foreign-born Cubans in the United States, thirteen thousand in New York City, eight thousand in Florida and a bit more than one thousand in California. It was in those years that Miami represented the Cuban American population center. Later on this number increased, the Census estimated that in 1960 there were eighty thousand foreign-born Cubans and forty thousand represented the second generation. These immigrants show a great diversity. In 1960 it was evident that the Cuban revolution decided to reshape Cuban society completely. Until the Cuban missile crisis of 1962 air transportation between the two countries worked very well. When this crisis happened, there were no direct flights between Cuba and the United States. The Johnson administration signed a "memorandum of understanding" with Castro's government at the end of 1965 that established a Cuban airlift to Miami; usually there was one flight every day. In 1973 more than 250000 Cubans arrived in the United States. In spite of the fact that the federal government tried to distribute the group throughout the country, the majority of Cubans have clustered in southern Florida, especially in Miami where they exercised a significant impact on the economic development and political life of the country. Out of the one million more than half million of this population live in southern Florida. Other Cubans are concentrated primarily in New York City, Newark, Los Angeles and Chicago.

Most Cuban Americans are at least from the lower middle class. A large number of white Cuban population lives in poor condition, especially the old generation and those in households which are headed by women. Black Cubans represent a significant number of the island population who have been underrepresented in the refugees who immigrated to the United States. Their financial position is worse than that of other Cubans who settled down in the Northeast.

Cuban Americans intend to return to their native-born country especially those among the earliest refugees. The Cuban American politics is different from that of Puerto Rican or Mexican American. They have essentially middle-class life styles and habits, and they think that they have hardly anything in common with other Spanish-speaking population.

3. OTHER SPANISH-SPEAKING GROUPS IN THE UNITED STATES

In addition to the major Spanish-speaking groups in the United States, there exists a number of isolated groups whose use of Spanish language has virtually no interaction with the remainder of the country's Spanish speakers. Only one tiny group whose use of Spanish is now close to extinction can be found in northwestern Louisana, on either side of the Sabine river.

3.1 Judeo-Spanish (Dzhudezmo)

The *Sephardic Jews*, especially those who arrived in the United States in the twentieth century, are spread throughout the country, but most of them cluster in New York City. There are no exact data about the total number of *Sephardic Jews* or the number of those people who still speak the dialect of *Judeo-Spanish* (it can be called "Ladino" or Dzhudezmo as well). According to R. Renald in the mid-sixties, there were about 15000 United States Ladino speakers in the country and it is very apparent that this variety of the language is very quickly losing its significance around there. Consequently, this dialect of the United States Spanish is disappearing, however, there are some linguistic descriptions accomplished concerning this language variety.

Major studies

There are researchers on the United States Dzhudezmo, with particular attention to phonology and vocabulary. Studies of New York Judeo-Spanish are the most prominent such as Luria's article on "Judeo Spanish dialects in New York City" (1930), or Agard's overview of phonology, morphology and lexicon and the two wide-ranging linguistic descriptions by R. Hirsch (1951) and D. Levy (1952) doctoral dissertations.

3.2 Louisansa Spanish: isleño

The speech of the isleños, early Canary Island colonists who settled down on the territory what is called Louisana, is an even sadder state of documentation. This dialect of Spanish was investigated by R. MacCurdy in the late 1940s, as reported in his dissertation (1948) and the publications derived therefrom. MacCurdy's work is within the Hispanic tradition, which lacks in an awareness of scientific linguistics. At the time of MacCurdy, the estimated number of the community was five thousand *isleño* Spanish speakers which by now has declined by half of this number.

3.2.1. Spanish loanwords in English by 1900

Spanish has been a major influence on the vocabulary of the English language during the last five decades. Recently, this influence has increased, primarily on the language of the United States and upon other varieties through it. Therefore, the influence of Spanish on the vocabulary of English is without doubt.

When we deal with the question of borrowing Spanish loanwords, we can make a difference between "immidiate" and "ultimate" sources:

On the one hand, English has borrowed Spanish words whose original source is not Spanish; that is to say that Spanish borrowed earlier from other languages like Amerindian varieties (such as barbecue from the Spanish barbacoa; from a Taino word for a framework of sticks). All kinds of words, whose immediate source is Spanish, are regarded as Spanish loans.

On the other hand, there are Spanish loanwords that English borrowed not directly from Spanish but from another language. For example, the Spanish and Portuguese words such as *veranda* or *baranda* (meaning balcony) were introduced first into Indic languages, which later entered the vocabulary of Anglo-Indian languages and finally came into general English use as "veranda". Despite its "ultimate" Iberian origin, the word is regarded as an Indic borrowing.

One main dilemma that occurs frequently is to decide whether a word entered English from Spanish or from one of the other Romance languages. The Arabic *nadir* was commonly used by European languages by the late middle ages. There is no clear evidence in which country the word was used first; in Italy, France, Spain or Portugal. Furthermore, we are not sure from which language the first user of the word borrowed it. Allegedly, Chaucer was the first person to use it, but it does not mean that he introduced the word into the English language. There are words, which were borrowed several times with the same or different meaning. For example, the word "Castilian" was used in English in 1526 as a label for a "Spanish gold coin". More than two decades later, it stood for a "native of Castile" and for "pertaining to Castile". The late eighteenth century general use has certainly nothing to do with the early sixteenth century specific use. The older use is now out of date, only the later one survives in contemporary English.

Similar examples are:

- *sombrero:* first in the sense of "parasol", later it was reborrowed but with the meaning of 'broad-brimmed hat'
- *gracioso*: first meant "court favourite" but later it stood for a buffon in a Spanish comedy
- *muchacho:* was first explained in the Oxford English Dictionary as a "boy-servant" in the Spanish army while the mid-nineteenth century American use must be a reborrowing, which is not directly related to the late sixteenth-century British use. This is a word that entered English several times but with different meanings.

There are English words like *marquisate*, which was composed on the model of other existing elements. In this case, this word was constructed on the basis of Spanish *marquesado*, French *marquisat* and Italian *marchesato*. The word is composed of two parts: "marquis" and the suffix "ate".

A loanword may develop new forms and senses in English. The question is whether the new uses are the same lexeme as the old one or new items. For example, Spanish *mondongo* (meaning "tripe") was borrowed in 1622, fifteen years later it appeared as *mundungus* (in a pseudo-Latin shape) with the meaning of "refuse", "garbage" and later in the sense of a "dark smelly potato". The question is whether these two forms represent the same word due to their common etymology or are different words because their forms and meanings are different.

There are loanwords which are evidently of foreign origin as regards spelling and pronunciation:

- *canon* is a more foreign spelling than *canyon*
- the pronunciation of *laso* as /læso/ is closer to Spanish than that of /læsu/ that is of English influence
- Both *ranch* and *rancho* came to English from Mexican Spanish but the former is less foreign than the latter owing to the lack of 'o' from the end of the word.

3.2.2. A chronological survey

The inflow of Spanish words into the English lexicon throughout the years has increased in quantity. In the fourteenth century the Spanish loanword *alkanet* "a red eye" entered English. Later on, other words came from a Romance source, which may have been Spanish or another related tongue: *brazil* and *nadir*.

At the beginning of the fifteenth century "crimson" entered English in the form of "cremesyn", but later this shape changed. "Seville" entered English as an attributive for oil first and later for oranges.

Especially in the sixteenth century Spanish loanwords in English increased very intensively. Among the 260 loanwords from Spanish during that century 106 are still current. The most important semantic categories among these loans are as follows:

- animals: *alcatras, alligator* (a reptile of crocodile family), *flamingo* (a bird of pink plumage), *mosquito* (blood-sucking, fly-like insect)

- plants, foodstuffs: *apricot* (an orange-colored fruit), *banana* (a fruit), *cacao* (the seed from which chocolate and cocoa are prepared), *maize* (Indian corn), *papaya* (a tropical fruit), *potato* (a sweet potato, an Irish potato)

- other foods and drinks: *lunch* (midday meal), *sherry*

- tobacco and drugs: *tobacco*

- human beings by occupation and qualities: *hidalgo* (a Spanish gentleman), *cavalier* (a horseman, a gentleman) , *mestizo* (a person of mixed blood), *mulatto* (one of the mixed race, especially white and black), *negro* (a black of American descent), *señora* (a title of respect for a Spanish lady)

- places and inhabitants: *Aragonese* (of Aragon), *Carib* (West Indian Native)

- government: *alcalde* (a Spanish town magistrate)

- clothing: *sombrero* (a hat)

- meteorology: *hurricane, savannah, tornado*

- travel and movement: *canoe*

- money: *peso*

- family and trades: *magazine*

On the basis of this collection there is no doubt that a lot of Spanish loanwords which derive from the sixteenth century are the result of the Spanish exploration of the New World and the transmission of knowledge of America through Spain and of terms for New World phenomena. The increasing influx of these loans is evidently due to the increased economic and political influence of Spain.

Throughout the next century Spanish influence remained strong; two loans out of three hundred are still in general use nowadays. In this period we can differentiate the following most important categories:

- animals: *albatross* (a large sea bird), *dorado* (a kind of fish), *llana* (a camel-like beast of burden)

- plants, foodstuffs or other products: *avocado* (a large pear-shaped fruit), *chilli* (a red pepper), *mangrove* (a kind of tree), *tomato* (a garden vegetable), *vanilla* (an orchid plant from which a flavoring is made)

- other foods and drinks: *vino* (wine), *barbecue* (a wooden frame for sleeping and cooking meat)

- human beings by occupation and qualities: *Doňa* (a courtesy title), *mulatta* (a female mulatto), *seňor* (a title of respect)

- places and inhabitants: *Asturian* (of Asturias), *Portuguese* (of Portugal), *Mexican* (of Mexico)

- architecture, construction: *alcazar* (a fortress), *plaza* (marketplace)

- crime and punishment: *desperado* (a desperate person)

- meteorology, topography: *llana* (a treeless plain in northern South America), *sierra* (a sawtoothed range of mountains)

- entertainment: *gracioso* (1. a court's favourite, 2. a buffoon in Spanish comedy)

- farming, trades: *cargo* (a ship's load), *embargo* (a prohibition against trade with a foreign country)

- miscellanous: *adios* (goodbye), *siesta* (an afternoon rest)

Eighteenth century loanwords among which seventy are still current fall into almost the same categories as the earlier ones:

- animals: *puma* (a cougar)
- plants, foodstuffs: *cocoa* (the seed of the cocoa tree, the powder made from it), *oregano* (wild marjoram, a reasoning)
- other foods and drinks: *sangria* (a cold punch of red wine and fruit juice)
- tobacco, drugs: *cigar* (a roll of tobacco leaves for smoking)
- human beings by occupation and qualities: *caballero* (a Spanish gentleman), *albino* (a person lacking bodily pigment)
- places, inhabitants: *Apache* (Amerindian people of the Southwest), *Castilian* (of Castile)
- topography: *pampa* (a treeless plain in the South of America), *cordillera* (a montain chain)
- entertainment: *bolero* (a Spanish dance or a music for it), *picador* (a mounted bullfighter who provokes the bull with a lance)

The nineteenth century was not the most productive era in the history of borrowings from Spanish into English. At that time about forty-six percent of the Spanish loanwords are still in general use today. 241 of the nineteenth-century loans are still current. The influx of loanwords is due to the linguistic contact between English and Spanish speakers in the American Southwest. Before the nineteenth century loans derive first of all from Spain, but recent borrowings are due to the influence of American Spanish on the English of the United States. At that time semantic areas of borrowings remained more or less the same as those of earlier times coupled with some new categories, one for example is related to cowboy culture:

- animals: *lobo, tuna*
- plants: *yerba buena, madroño*
- foods and drinks: *aguardiente, chorizo, Cuba libre, fino, gazpacho, salsa, tequila*

- tobacco and drugs: *cigarillo, Corona, marijuana*
- deseases: *loco*
- human beings by occupation and qualities: *amigo, hombre, señorita*
- places, inhabitants: *Argentine, Dominician, Madrileño*
- architecture, buildings, construction: *barrio, pueblo*
- agression, military: *conquistador, guerilla*
- crime and punishment: *bad man*
- clothing, cosmetics: *mascara*
- meteorology, topography: *arroyo, canyon, playa*
- entertainment: *aficionado, fiesta, flamenco*
- money: *centavo, dinero, peseta*
- cowboys, cattle: *rancho, rodeo, vaquero*
- miscellaneous: *bonanza* (an unexpected benefit), *caramba* (an exclamation of surprise or alarm), *mañana* (tomorrow), *vamoose* (to leave)

4. PRESENT-DAY SPANISH IN AMERICAN ENGLISH

4.1 Recent borrowings from Spanish into English (Garland Cannon)

4.1.1. Background

Until the Barnharts' publication of the first major new-word dictionary in English (1973), there was no reliable evidence concerning the different kinds of new items which have entered the modern English vocabulary. After this publication, Merriam alphabetized into a unique list all items added in the Addenda Sections since the original publication of *Webster's Third*, and published these as *6000 Words*. Later this was followed by larger collections *(9000 Words, 12000 Words)*. Meanwhile, the Barnharts published a second collection which was followed by the *Third Bernhart Dictionary of New English* (1990).

It could be predicted that Barnhart and Merriam would not take other dialects of English (British, South-African, Australian, etc.) into consideration except for Canadian English owing to the proximity of Canada to the United States. Canadian English is closer to the American dialect of English than any other variety and has added some extra words to Canadian English, too. Meanwhile, computerization of the data in the richest sources of English words was completed at the University of Waterloo (Toronto). Two Waterloo computer retrievals were required to collect Spanish terms. The first run in 1991 retrieved thirty-eight items which were etymologized as Spanish. The second run retrieved items from 1950 which were etymologized as Mexican Spanish or American Spanish.

(Gonzáles, 1996:31)

While there was no duplication between the two lists, citations from the pre-1950 period in other sources reduced the total to eighty-six items. Apparently, all of these items are considered to be of Spanish origin. These items turned up later than 1949, among which at least three may be familiar to scholars due to the fact that these were already widely used in *Webster's Third* for which there were citations earlier which Barnharts found. Furthermore, Burchfield and the new-word dictionaries record more than twenty items from the 1950s that are not used in *Webster's Third* and are based on current, mainly American Spanish loans.

One of the most serious problems that are to be dealt with is that twenty-four items appear in *Burchfield dictionary* but not in *Webster's Third* are earlier than 1950. These items are not really used by scholars, or evenmore, they do not know these items. Almost all of them except for the adjective *hacienda* are recorded in at least one new-word dictionary, which suggests that lexicographers who made this list regarded the items as borrowings or revivals of previous borrowings. This means that an item may have some early citations, which then disappears in English for a long time but later suddenly reappears. The way to solve the mystery is to exclude revivals from the corpus which are not chronologically new but to list them together with other pre-1950 items according to their earliest date: *bota, tornillo, parador, Piña Colada, El Niňo, rancho, ranchito, Hispano, macho, machismo, etc.*

(Cannon, 1995:54)

4.1.2. Semantic categories of Spanish

The semantic categories into which Spanish corpus can be divided are considerably different from those of other languages.

The largest semantic categories of French are food and the arts, or in the case of Japan these are arts and material arts.

The picture in Spanish is different: the leading category here is politics (thirty-nine items) then food and drink (twenty items) and the third category is related to status or occupation (twelve items), while sociology represents the forth largest category (nine items). In the category of sport there are eight items, usually connected to bullfighting which is the most dominant of Spanish sports. In this category the most peculiar item is *matadora*. As for the ethnological items are concerned, three of them derive from the same root *(Chicana, Chicanismo, Chicano)*. Other categories such as music or narcotics consist of five items, while linguistics, military and theology contain four items each.

4.1.3. Vocabulary

Four reborrowings transfer meanings, which are considerably different from the original such as *coyote*, which has an interesting history. First it was used in the sense of "predator animal" (1759), later in the sense of "slouching fellow", Indian or "mestizo" (1872). This latter meaning is used in a negative sense: someone who exploits immigrants illegally from the countries of Latin America or the United States.

Salsa "an energetic dance or music" can be distantly related to its original sense: "a hot sauce".

The language of the United States is without doubt much more influenced by the Spanish language of Latin America than by European Spanish. The term American Spanish covers almost each varieties of Spanish in Latin America; such as Spanish in the Antilles or Spanish in Central and South America. Mexican Spanish is a bit different from the others as a result of Indian influences. Notable instances are the loss of one or more elements in *contrarevolucionario, el Niňo, quiniela perfecta*. These are such cases when articles before Spanish nouns are lost like in *Bunker,* the Spanish definite male article *el* disappears. In this case there are two important exceptions: *la huya, la raza.*

4.1.4. The language of La Raza

The language of *La Raza* is more than a "hybrid language" that unites English and Spanish. It is a new language with a distinctive vocabulary, its own borrowed and re-created grammar, and a unique usage, which combines the Castilian Spanish of the conquerors and the frontier Americanism of English with the ancient and modern languages like Indians. One aspect of this "language" is *Pachucho* which is neither Spanish, nor English but instead the creation of barrios. *Placa* for police cannot be traced to the popular Mexican *placa* with the meaning of "baggage check", or the old Spanish *placa* that means "star or insignia of knights", nor any English equivalents. *Placa* according to Santamaría *Diccionario de mejicanismos* (1959) (Dictionary of Mexicanisms) does not mean "baggage check" in Mexico but rather *lámina pequeña con rótulo o inscripción...para vehiculos con número de registro o de orden, etc.* (a little picture with label or inscription...for vehicle of plate or orden number, etc.)

(Steiner, 1982:41)

> *"Even the proper Spanish spoken in the barrios is not truly Spanish. It never was. Words that are used in everyday life like tortilla (omelet) or chilli are of course not Spanish at all, but are from the languages of the Mexican Indians..."*

(Steiner, 1982: 41)

Nearly all Americans agree that they belong to the *La Raza,* which is a term connoting not racial but ethnic solidarity, and a sense of common destiny. Unfortunately, these terms do not provide a convenient adjective to identify members of the group. Clearly Mexican Americans is the identification that is most widely used and accepted today.

4.1.5. Grammar

Nouns of Spanish origin do not have irregular plurals. There are only two nouns of double plurality: *frijoles y refritos* (refried beans), *huevos rancheros* (fried eggs). These two instances do not cause disturbance in the English inflectional system as they were borrowed as ready-made plurals. Since the items such as *numero uno* (number one) or *Cinco de Mayo* (the fifth of May) are mass nouns, they are not pluralized. If they were, a monolingual English speaker would say rather *numero unos* than *numeros unos.*

4.1.6. Phonology

When the phonology of the two languages is similar to each other, we can anticipate the great majority to be phonetic transfers. In this way, seven of Spanish etyma are transferred with the suffix *–ismo-* (Chicanismo), only *Fidelism* appears as paired, anglisized form an *latifundism* appears without its paired, Spanish form.

The case is similar with the suffix *–ista-,* only two having a paired anglicized form: *Fidelist, latifundist.*

The Spanish grammatical form is preserved in four feminine items like *Chicano-Chicana, santero-santera, matador-matadora* and *Latino-Latina*.

4.1.7. Productivity

English is a very productive language in every respect, even in the case of Spanish borrowings as well:

- *refry* has been backformed from refried beans
- *contra* can function as a noun referring to someone especially from the right wing, who opposes another
- from the word *perfecta* other words can be formed by adding the following prefixes: *-super-*, and *–by-* (*superfecta, trifecta*)

4.1.8. Well-known newly borrowed Spanish terms

- *Burrito:* the name of a meal
- *Chicana:* female Chicano
- *Cinco de Mayo:* a Mexican holiday celebrating a French military defeat
- *huelga:* strike
- *matadora:* a woman matador
- *tourista:* tourist

Productive forms:

Acapulco Gold, banana belt, chili dog, Zapata mustache, tequila sunrise, guerilla theater, Columbian gold

4.2 Ethnic nicknames of Spanish origin in American English

Hispanics were not only the discoverers and colonizers of the southern part of the United States, but they were also the founders of the two oldest towns: *St. Augustine* (Florida) and *Santa Fe* (New Mexico). Spanish influence can be seen in the name of the following states: *Nevada* (meaning snowy), *Florida* (meaning flowery) and *Montana* (meaning montainous), in the name of the cities: *Los Angeles, San Francisco, San Diego, Los Alamos, Tijuana* (near the Mexican border), *Amarillo, San*

Angelo, San Antonio, in the denomination of montains: *Sierra Blanca, Sierra Gorda, Sierra Nevada* and in the name of lakes and rivers: *Laguna Madre, Rio Grande.*

American people use Spanish loanwords and phrases with a very high frequency, especially concerning food and beverage: *Cuba libre, arroz con pollo* (rice with chicken), *frijoles* (beans), *tequila, tortilla* (omelet), *taco, paella, burrito.*

Americans also adapt Hispanic traditions, habits like "Paella festival", "the parade of the three kings in Miami", "the Posadas in California" or the "Piñata parties" in San Antonio.

Those expressions in the United States are also widely-used which came into the language from Indian languages through Spanish: *barbecoe, canoe, hurricane, maize, savannah, avocado, cacao, coyote, tomato, tequila.*

After the second world war Spanish-speaking people were asked whether they were Spanish or not; with this question referring not to their native language but to countries where they came from. The language of the Castilian Spanish was regarded as the standard variety of Spanish while American Spanish was the sub-standard dialect.

Terms such as "Latinos", "Latin Americans", "Hispanics" and "Hispanic Americans" won popularity in the 1970s. "Latinos" was the broadest category including every Romance language speaker of the world. The definition of "Latino-Americans" was restricted to those who were born in the southern hemisphere. The term "Hispanics" was coined from the adjective "Hispanic"; both labels deriving from the name "Hispania" referring to Spain. From a logical point of view, the meaning of "Hispanics" is anything that has something to do with Spain, to its language or culture. The label "Hispanic Americans" is the narrowest category of all: this name refers to those whose language and customs are of Spanish origin and who were born on the continent. This name does not only cover Spanish speakers in Hispanic American nations but also Spanish speakers in the United States.

In the United States of America the Census requires information about race. The choices are the followings: Black, Caucasian, Hispanic, Asian, Native American etc. This mixture of race and ethnicity is confusing to those Hispanic people who are

Caucasian or Black or Chinese or Japanese or Indian, but all of whom are of Hispanic American origin.

A lot of signs can be found in public places or cars:

> "*Do not call me a Hispanic; I am a Cuban, a Mexican or Puerto Rican!*"

With regard to Anglo-Americans, *blancos, blanquillos, bolillos, gabachos* are pejorative nicknames referring to ethnicity used in the Southwest. In Mexican and Central American Spanish the preferred word in the same sense is *gringos* while in Caribbean English it is *yankees*.

There are several interesting and imaginative hypotheses concerning the origin of the word *gringo*. According to one of the most popular hipotheses, the word derives from "green grow". This word was considered to be a synonym of "foreigner", "stranger" during the eighteenth and nineteenth centuries in Spain. Coromimas, a Spanish theoritician, derives the word from *griego* (Greek) which was often used in Spain in the phrase: *hablar en griego* but not with the meaning of "speaking Greek" but with that of "incomprehensible language". The result is that English speakers today often apply the expression "that is Greek" in the sense of something being unclear for them. However, the equivalent Spanish meaning of this expression is *eso es chino* – "that is Chinese" (in word for word translation).

On the other hand, the expressions such as *hablar en griego* or *hablar en gringo* are still in popular use in a lot of South American countries; meaning "talking gibberish".

The word *gringo* has undergone a great number of semantic changes. According to Corominas, the most accepted connotation in Spain is that of "incomprehensible language", or as stated above, it can be attributed to foreigners. On the other hand, in American Spanish the word refers to persons not to the language. In countries such as Argentina, Paraguay and Urugay people with this word referred to European immigrants especially to Italians who represented the largest ethnic minority group in these countries. Nowadays, the use of this word is restricted to English speakers without any offensive meaning. However, in Central America and Mexico the case is different: in these two countries the term defines a "blond person" whose hair color is not typical of the inhabitants of these countries and is very strange for the native dwellers.

Nowadays, *gringo* is considered to be a standard word in both Spanish and English, from which several compounds and derivatives have been formed: *griganda, gringaje* (a group of gringos), *gringuito* (a small American child), *gringofobia* (dislike of foreigners). One of the most preferred ethnic names for those Chicanos who try to adapt themselves to American habits and customs is the use of the term *coco* (coconut). This word may refer to a Chicano who marries an Anglo-Saxon citizen with a derigatory connotation.

Other ways of satirizing Chicanos is referring to them as *cholo, pachucho, pelado* or *pocho*. The only term which is not derigatory for them is *Texmex.* With this name we mean a Chicano who is from Texas. All of the above terms except for this are pejorative; their use is restricted to the English of the Southwest and California.

Cholo is a "mestizo", *pelado* is an ill-bred, vulgar person while for the origin of *pachucho* there is no confirmed theory. According to some theoriticians, the term could derive from the Mexican city of *Pachucha.* This term is not widely used but its derivative *pachuquismo* is popular in Mexican Spanish, which is defined as linguistic peculiarities of the dialect *pachucho*.

The theoritician *Santamaria* states that the word *poche* is used in California and in the southern states of the United States, but in Mexico the word has a slightly different form: *pocho*.

Santamaría with this term refers to the North Americans of Spanish origin especially those from Mexico. When a Mexican American mixes English and Spanish, he is considered to be a "pochista". "Pochismo" is another Mexican-American term standing for "chicanismo" or "Spanglish".

Mexican Americans are often called "tirilones". This label refers to troublemakers, gangs, juvenile deliquents, drug addicts, which has the variants "tirili" and "trilongo" with the same meaning.

Puerto Ricans living in New York City and in other cities of New Jersey are proud of their nickname "borincano" or "borinqueño" because these are gentilic nouns derived from "Borinquen" – the Taino Indian name for Puerto Rico. The term "negro" is of Spanish origin, which is related to black people. Since it is a very offensive connotation for them, nowadays the term "Negro" has been replaced by the denotations of "black", "Afro-American", "African-American". These are labels to be of preferred use today since these are not connected to the cruel period of slavery.

Cubans have been immigrating to the United States since the early 1700s, whose dialect has had an important impact on the English of Florida.

Cuban Americans have introduced several ethnic nicknames into English, some with a slight change of meaning. For example *Cubanazo* before Castro referred to a honest, industrious Cuban person. Nowadays, by this term we mean a Cuban who feels and acts as though he were "Tarzan". From this several other words have been formed such as *cubanear, cubaneo* and *cubaneria*, which have become part of the English dialect spoken in Florida. *Cubanear* is a verb meaning "act like a Cuban" while *cubaneo* and *cubaneria* refer to "behaving according to the typical characteristic features of the Cubans": being happy, laughing a lot, being noisy, talking a lot.

Spanish, such as English is very abundant in derivational processes coupled with its ingenuity and the humor of its speakers are worth mentioning. This may explain why there are so many nicknames in this language.

4.3 Spanish place names in the United States

The existence of Spanish place names in the southern and western parts of the country proves that once these states were parts of the "Spanish Borderlands". Spanish place names belong to two large categories: commemorative and descriptive names. Commemorative names are usually proper nouns, very often referring to the names of saints and liturgical festivals of the Catholic Church, namely, that Hispanics are Chatolics by religion.

Descriptive names are common nouns that refer to the characteristic features of the territory. Among the commemorative names *San Agustine* in Florida was anglicized as *Saint Augustine;* the inhabitants of San Francisco strongly oppose any abbreviations for the city like: *"Do not call it Frisco!",* Los Angeles is a shortened form of its original name: *Nuestra Señora de Los Angeles de Porciuncula*.

The number of the place names of the descriptive category is abundant: *Mesa Verde, Blue Mesa, Grand Mesa* which are in the state of Colorado (*mesa* meaning flat-topped mountain); *Arroyo de Colorado, Arroyo de Muerto Arroyo Seco* in New Mexico (arroyo meaning stream).

Some place names for instance *Rio de las Plumas* were translated into English; the translation of this particular phrase is *Feather River.* On the other hand, there are many place names which are maintained in their original shape such as *Las Vegas, Los Alamos, La Jolla, Dos Palos, El Cerrito*, etc. In the case of these settlements it is evident that the definite article or a similar modifier is involved. Some other names like *Rio Grande* or *Rio Colorado* do not contain the definite article or any other modifier, but they are normally translated into English: *Grand River* and *Colorado River. Buena Vista* that is found in the Colorado Rockies has an authentic Spanish syntactic pattern: Adjective+Noun. However, in general use *vista* "view" appears in Noun+Noun constructions such as *Rio Vista* in New Mexico, which in English means "river new". In California similar phrases can be found: *Valle Vista, Sierra Vista* – "valley view", "range view".

Other peculiarity concerning place names is the conversion of Spanish adjectives into full-fledged place names: the adjectival modifier in *Rio Colorado* provided the name of the state, the town of *Chico* in California received its name from *Arroyo Chico* (meaning little stream) while the denomination of the state *Nevada* derives from *Sierra Nevada*.

4.3.1. Background

The Southwest in the United States consists of five states: *California, Arizona, New-Mexico, Colorado* and *Texas*. These territories were ceded by the United States after their triumph against the Mexicans as a result of the Treaty of Guadalupe Hidalgo. Among the Hispanic groups, the Mexicans constitute the largest number of Spanish-speaking population in the United States. Their number is estimated to be ten million Mexican Americans. Since the United States is regarded as a multicultural country, it is evident that there are many other nationalities living there; especially, those of the immigrants from Europe and from other continents. The co-existence of the two cultures, namely, Anglo-American and Hispanic gave rise to the existence of a mixed culture.

Within the Spanish continuum we can make a difference between four subdialects:

- *Standard Mexican Spanish*

- *New Mexican Spanish* that was introduced by the conquerors in the sixteenth century. This variety is spoken in the areas of northern New-Mexico and southern Colorado.

- *The Southwest dialect* (Mexican American or Chicano Spanish) is the mixed Spanish, which is influenced by the English language to a large extent.

- The dialect which is also of considerable importance is an argot: *Chicano Caló*, which developed as "Pachucho" in the el Paso area and is the street language of the teenagers. This language variety was transported to the New World from Mexico City to the United States Southwest. Such as Black English in the North, *Chicano Caló* through metaphor and suffixation is employed in the Southwest to express humor, exaggeration, outrage *machismo* and other effects.

The English continuum includes the following varieties:

- *Standard American English* with southern and northern varieties

- *Southwest* English within which there are certain number of subdialects

- Finally, the language variety that is used especially by bilinguals is *The Mexican American English*.

The Southwest reflects a so-called "state-bilingualism" as a result of heavy legal and illegal immigration to the territory. There are other aspects of bilingualisms, as well such as "incipient bilingualism", this type of bilingualism is characteristics of those individuals whose mother tongue is English and did not master Spanish perfectly.

The third type does not differ very much from that of the "incipient type" while in case of the forth type, namely, "passive bilingualism", the comprehension skill of the speakers is far better than that of speaking.

The existence of diglossia is again a peculiarity of Spanish-English bilingualism, according to which Spanish performs primarily the informal and low functions of communication concerning the contexts of family, friendship, religion; whereas English occupies the high function such as official, legal, educational, commercial and literary-aesthetic functions.

4.3.2. Directions of borrowing

According to conventional wisdom, the directions of borrowing occurs vertically; from the "dominant language" above the "subordinate" one below. The language of the United States have borrowed a lot of Spanish words from the area of drugs and addiction. It is well-known that many serious drugs originate in South and Central America which spread through Spanish-speaking countries to the United States.

American English lexicon is also influenced by Mexican Spanish to a great extent in the fields of ranching, breeding, agriculture, fauna and flora and a kind of "idealized world of romance" with beautiful *señoritas* and good-looking *caballeros*.

The accepted belief as stated above is that borrowing first of all occurs vertically, but in cases of stable bilingualism a kind of "horizontal borrowing" develops which means that both languages borrow words from each other but not necessarily in a great quantity.

The theoriticians *George Green* and *Lino García* stated in their essay that English loanwords borrowed by Spanish are usually from the public sphare whereas Spanish terms, expressions borrowed by English are from private domains because in the southern part of the United States near the Mexican border Spanish is the language in the majority of homes. Green and García discussed some terms and grouped into the following three categories:

- Food: *chilli, tortilla, paella*

- Social arrangement: *quinceañera* (a party for girls of fifteen), *tornaboda* (a little night continuation of a wedding party for family or friends)

- Extended family: *padrino* (godfather), *ahijado* (godchild), *tio* (uncle)

4.3.3. Code-switching, code shifting

Bilingual conversation in the Southwest reflects very interesting phenomena. If the speaker in a dialogue is from ethnicity, the Southwestern Spanish dialect is applied in the conversation; evenmore, switching between Spanish and English is abundant. However, if the speaker's Spanish knowledge is not sufficient, the conversation continues in English.

Among Chicano speakers code-switching is a very complex process because this involves not only shifting from one language to another but from one level of meaning to another.

Undoubtedly, switching is dominant first of all in oral speech but it can occur in the literary works of the Southwest, as well; especially by Chicano authors. They write either in Spanish or English but very often employ both of these in one work.

4.3.4. Southwest-vocabulary in major English dictionaries

The following two categories concerning the vocabulary of the Southwest are noteworthy:

- *Southwest flora*
- *folk or popular medicine* or sometimes referred to as *ethno-medicine*

These two areas seem to be tightly connected to each other to a large extent, namely, that a lot of plants serve popular medicinal purposes.

Another peculiar item in the Southwest common vocabulary that is worth mentioning is the unique *luminarias* "Southwest Christmas lights" (consisting of paper bags, sand, candles, it is glowing for days).

Taking into consideration the colloquial or even "hybrid" nature of Southwest lexicon, it can be expected that many words of this type are omitted from the famous English dictionaries like *American Heritage Dictionary, Webster's Third New International Dictionary* and *Oxford English Dictionary*. Some items in connection with Southwesternern culture and topography are included in these dictionaries: *viga* "beam", was listed only in Webster's dictionary whereas *arroyo* "dry gulch", *agave* "family of tropical plants", *alamo* "cottonwood", *palo verde* "desert tree" were collected in all of these three.

Surprisingly enough, the term *luminarias* cannot be found in any of the three dictionaries.

4.3.5. Some well-known items from the lexicon of the Southwest

Finally, I have listed the most popular words and expressions that are used in the Southwest today:

- *amá:* Mom, Má
- *andale:* let's go, OK
- *apá:* Dá
- *arme:* army, armed services

- *borlo:* dance, party
- *bote:* jail, prison
- *bute:* a lot, much, very
- *chao:* hello, goodbye (from the Italian *ciao*)
- *chamba:* work, job (this noun comes from the verb *chambiar* 'to work')
- *hola:* hello, hi
- *huevos:* balls, guts
- *jefa:* old lady, mother
- *jefe:* old man, father
- *mano:* brother, friend
- *mamasota:* beautiful woman
- *no problemo:* no problem
- *onda:* occurence, trend; *Qué onda?* meaning What is happening?
- *padrísimo:* super, fantastic
- *pantas:* pants, trousers
- *papás:* parents
- *parna:* partner
- *tecato:* drug addict, alcoholic
- *totacho, totacha:* speech, language
- *vacil:* fun, laughs

5. SPANISH TERMS IN AMERICAN LITERATURE

5.1 Introduction

The racism and ignorance concerning Mexican-Americans is a very important characteristic feature of the early American literature. The majority of Spanish words in American literature concern the Mexican-Americans. The writers of the mid-nineteenth century American literature tried to characterize their heroes in their work: they are beautiful and young *señoritas* who are pure Spanish; on the other hand, males are regarded as dirty Mexicans, not pure Spanish, neither pure Indians but mixed creatures.

5.2 William Sidney Porter (introduction)

This person is generally known as O. Henry, who is originally from North-Carolina. He spent many years of his life in Texas where he got to know the Spanish language, learnt it first of all from the Mexican Americans, secondly, through a Spanish book. O. Henry used a lot of Spanish terms and expressions in his stories about the frontier country. His most famous character is *Cisco Kid* the story of which is abundant in Spanish words: Cisco Kid, who is a bad *hombre* (man), has a girlfriend whose name is *Tonia Pérez.* She is living between *Frio* and *Rio Grande.* The name of *Tonia* derives from Antonia. Throughout the story, O. Henry continues using a lot of Spanish words such as *pantalones, camisa, tienda, frijoles, caballero, dios* (trousers, shirt, shop, beans, chavalier, gods).

5.3 O. Henry's poetry

O. Henry is not only a good author but he is also an excellent poet, whose most popular poem concerning *Mexicanos* is "Tamales".

Even the title of the poem is Spanish, the work itself is full of Spanish and English words and expressions. On the English terms Spanish influence is strong, and there are Spanish words in the poem, which are very similar to their English equivalents:

Tamales

This is the Mexican

Don José Calderón

One of God's countrimen

Land of the buzzard.

Cheap silver dollar, and

Cacti and murdererers.

Why he has left his land

Land of the lazy man,

Land of the pulque Land of the bull flight,

Fleas and revolution.

This is the reason, Hark to the wherefore;

Listen and tremble.

One of his ancestors,

Ancient and garlickly,

Probably grandfather, Died with boots on.

Killed by the Texans, Texans with big guns,

At San Jacinto,

Died without benefit

Of priest and clergy;

Died of minie balls, mescal and pepper

Don José Calderón

Heard of the tragedy

Heard of it, thought of it,

Vowed a deep vengeance,

Vowed retribution

On the Americans

Murderous gringos,

> *Especially Texans.*
>
> *"Valga me Dios!" que*
>
> *Ladrones, diablos,*
>
> *Matadores, mentidores,*
>
> *Caraccos y perros,*
>
> *Voy a matarles,*
>
> *Con solo mis manos,*
>
> *Toditas sin falta.*
>
> *Thus swore the hidalgo*
>
> *Don José Calderón.*
>
> ...
>
> *This is your deep revenge,*
>
> *You have greased all of us,*
>
> *Greased a whole nation*
>
> *With your Tamales,*
>
> *Don José Calderón,*
>
> *Santos Espiritión,*
>
> *Vincente Camillo,*
>
> *Quintana de Ríos,*
>
> *De Rosa y Ribera.*
>
> (Details from the poet *Tamales* written by O. Henry)

The main character of the poem is a male whose name is Don José Calderón. In most of the literary works as written about, the main characteristic features of Spanish-speaking males are negative; in this case Don José Calderón, who left his country.

The first part of the poem is not abundant in Spanish expressions, the only exception is the name *Don José Calderón* which is of Spanish origin. The second peculiarity in this stanza is that there is a reference to a great Spanish custom: bullfighting *(land of the bullfight).*

In the second stanza the author refers to *Texans* and to a name of a city in Texas: *San Jacinto*. Still in this part English labels are dominant, however, there are some English words of Spanish influence: *ancestor* "anciano" or "anciana" as a noun, *ancient* "anciano" or "anciana" as an adjective, *probably* "probablamente".

The only Spanish word that can be found in this part is in the last line: *mescal*. Going on with the poem, we get to know how Don José Calterón vowed a vengeance on the murderous *gringos* for murdering his grandfather in the battle of *San Jacinto*. English words of Spanish influence in this part are: "vengeance" *venganza* and "devil" *diablo*. In chapter **4.2.** *Ethnic nicknames in the United States* (see page 50.), the meaning and origin of the term *gringo* has been already explained: 'foreign and strange'. Here with this term O. Henry referred to the Texan people. In the following lines more and more Spanish words and expressions make the poem more interesting. Even the first exclamation can catch the eye: *"Valga me Dios!"* Then come continuously a mass of English words, all with negative meanings:

"Voy a matarles,"	"I am going to kill them"
"Con solo mis manos"	"With my own hand"
"Toditas sin falta"	"Without exception"

Only the line before last contains an expression of English-Spanish mixture:

"Thus swore the Hidalgo	'Thus swore the noble
Don José Calderón."	Don José Calderón."

Until this point it could be seen that in the beginning, the poem was abundant in English words and phrases and lacked in Spanish expressions, but further on Spanish became more and more dominant on English. The case is similar in the last stanza of the poem where Spanish proper names are prevalent:

>"Don José Calderón,
>
>Santos Esperetión,
>
>Vincente Camillo,
>
>Quintana de Ríos,
>
>De Rose y Ribera."

5.4 Summary

Spanish words, expressions, which are used in American literature take many forms which are dependant on the author, his knowledge and fluency of Spanish. To understand such poems, at least an intermediate level of knowledge of both Spanish and English is required.

6. SECOND LANGUAGE ACQUISITION, ERROR ANALYSIS

6.1 Introduction

Research on second language acquisition was first conducted within the framework of contrastive analysis. Contrastive analysis is not really concerned about the nature of language learning, however, it has been indispensable in the prediction of errors and the areas of difficulty in language learning. Error analysis deals with errors that learners commit as a result of their lack of knowledge of the target language.

6.2 Error analysis

In the following investigation three tests were examined which were written by students whose mother tongue is English and learn Spanish. These students were given enough time to complete their tasks but they were not allowed to review their answers when they were ready. They were not permitted to use dictionaries or textbooks. Furthermore, they were not told what types of structures were the purposes of the study, they were only asked to complete the tests in the best way they could and they were informed that the results of their efforts might help other learners. There were three kinds of tasks: translation, Grammaticality Judgements and fill-in the blank. Translation was administered first which avoided turning the attention of the students towards specific structures. Since fill-in the blank was the most transparent task (concerning both the structures and lexical items used in target constructions), it was checked last.

6.2.1. Translation

This task contained fifty items, which included examples of several relative constructions. The types of tasks were taken from two novels written by American authors and from a sociology textbook. Two students whose native language was English were enlisted to ensure that in spite of short and incomplete sentences, all of these sounded natural. The Spanish word was supplied for these lexical items, whose Spanish equivalents was probably unfamiliar to the students.

Furthermore, they were told to leave an empty space if they could translate a particular word, but they were compelled to give a translation for the remaining part of the sentence. In this way, even the beginners had more chance to provide better results because they were able to translate correctly even if they did not know the meaning of some words.

6.2.2. Grammatically Judgement task

This test is also made up of fifty items. Sixteen out of fifty contain correct samples of the structures of interest in the present study. The order of presentation of the different structures was randomized. Some sentences were taken from compositions, vocabulary was carefully selected to avoid problems which are usually connected to the unfamiliarity of lexical items; the variety of terms, moods, adverbs, adjectives and types of constructions were reduced to a minimum. The main purpose here was to present sentences that are not complicated and sound natural to any speaker of Spanish.

The task of the students was to find errors and correct them. Moreover, their second task was to give a proper English translation for the sentences.

6.2.3. Fill-in the blank

This test consists of forty-two items. Students were asked to fill in the blanks with appropriate relative words or conjunctions. Taking into consideration those students of beginning level as in the case of previous tests, elementary vocabulary was selected which helped them to understand better the meaning of the sentences.

6.2.4. Subjects

In this investigation fifty students were involved: forty-five out of the fifty were university students whose mother tongue was English, the remaining five were native Spanish speakers. They were grouped into the following categories:

- The first group consisted of the beginners who were fifteen university students. They had not been taught before how to form Spanish relative constructions or what lexical items were to be used in relatives. They had been learning Spanish for seven months.

- The second contained students of intermediate and advanced level. The number of them was fifteen each. They were in the second and third year Spanish courses at the University of Toronto.

- This was the control group, which consisted of those five students whose mother tongue was Spanish. They were from Spain and had been learning English in Spain and had already graduated from the university. They had been in Canada for almost two years and their knowledge of English was pretty good.

6.3 Results

The results of the three tests were coded and entered into computer files which have been categorized into three groups:

- determination of lexical items
- the status of the rules that determine the structure of the complementizer
- the status of language specific rules and constructions

6.3.1. Lexical items

Students applied the Spanish item *que* both as a complementizer and as a relative pronoun. In the three tests it was used between forty-six and sixty-four percent of the time by those students who were Spanish learners and only between thirty-seven and forty-one percent of the time by the control group. From this it can be seen that there are significant differences between native and non-native grammar. This difference may be due to the fact that *que* occurs very frequently in Spanish as a (1) complementizer with the same function as English "that", (2) as an interrogative meaning "what", (3) as a relative pronoun or (4) as a part of relative *el que*. All of these facts prove that *que* is a very productive lexical item.

What is even more surprising is the frequent use of *el que* by the English native speakers instead of *quien, el qual* or even *que*. This is an item, which occurs frequently in free relatives and cleft constructions.

The reason why beginners used *el que* so frequently in the "translation" and "fill-in the blank" exercises may be due to the influence of their knowledge of French or the fact that it was present in the "Grammaticality Judgements" task.

El que is regarded as a very special sequence primarily by the intermediate or advanced groups. The latter group favoured the use of *quien* but this rate is practically equal in the case of beginners and intermediate group. Moreover, nine beginners, six students of intermediate level and three of the advanced level used *que* after *durante* (during). This shows that they are in the process of learning that *que* can be used only after monosyllabic prepositions.

In the composition of the intermediate students there are very few instances of *el que* in spite of the fact that they had been taught how the different relative forms were used by native speakers. The advanced students preferred to use *quien* or *que*. *El cual* is more frequently used by language learners than by native speakers who prefer using *el que* to using *el cual*.

The item *cuyo* (whose, of which) does not belong to the grammar of the beginners. It is true that they knew the interrogatives but *cuyo* is not an interrogative in Spanish. Altogether only six instances were found in the blank-filling exercise and three in the translation task produced by this group but only two learners who are of Italian origin and have learnt this language at the university. Some strategies of the beginners to translate "whose" in the translation task are as follows:

- Buscaba a la muchacha quien tiene un padre que enseña portugués.

  I was looking for a girl who has a father that teaches Portuguese.

- Es la ciudad del nombre que no me recuerdo

  It is the city of the name that I do not remember.

- Es la muchacha de quien...

  It is the girl of whom...

The adverbials *cuándo* and *dónde* "when", "where" are used more frequently by the beginners in the translation task than in the others. These items belong to their grammar because these are also interrogatives.

6.3.2. The neuter strategy: the COMP structure

In this investigation the neuter strategy applies for translation and bank-filling exercises. This is used by the three learner groups at the same frequency; however, in the Grammaticality Judgements task the picture was different: whenever *que* was not present, either a noun phrase or nothing was produced. From the fact that few noun phrases are used by the three groups, the conclusion can be drawn that Non-native Grammar like native Spanish grammar applies the neuter strategy. Nevertheless, the Grammaticality Judgements task demonstrates that there was no definite judgement as the obligatoriness of *que* is concerned. In fact there was no difference between the three groups in the production of the noun phrases. Maybe it is due to the fact that the neuter strategy is not compulsory in non-restrictive clauses.

6.3.3. Empty COMP

Two instances of empty COMP were produced by an intermediate student:

- El tiempo _____ alguién espera a otra persona

  The time _____ somebody is waiting for another person

- para el tiempo _____ él está esperando

  for the time _____ he is waiting

In spite of the fact that there were a large number of test items containing this structure, the number of empty COMP structure produced in the translation task was small. Different students had produced different solutions that show that their translation is word by word and they did not check the final output.

Time complements

The three learners produced *que* and *cuando* as time complements. They did not really use prepositional phrases even when the stimulus was a prepositional phrase. There is a difference between the control group and the users of non-native grammar as far as the use of prepositional phrase versus adverbs is concerned. No cases like the following were produced:

- El día el que/el cual tu naciste.

  The day which you were born.

This instance proves that *el que* and *el cual* do not have the same status as *que* or *quien* in non-native grammar.

6.3.4. Language specific constructions

6.3.4.1 Preposition stranding

This construction was considered to be grammatical by almost half of the beginners in the Grammaticality Judgements exercise but they also insisted in this structure in the translation task. The type of the preposition or the type of the relative construction apparently did not influence the results. The advanced students did not accept this construction. When one of them was asked why she had not accepted it, she answered that she would never strand a preposition when learning another language because she had learnt that constructions like this were not "proper" English, nor was it used by native speakers. One person from the control group argued that she would never apply this type of construction because she had the impression that constructions like these are very strange: "a kind of idiom".

There were five cases of preposition copy by students from each group when they translated English sentences, which contained preposition stranding as in the following examples:

- de las que se oye hablar de - *which one hears to talk about*
- con que solía dormir con cuando era niño – *whith which used to sleep with when was child*
- de las que odiaba tan de hablar – *about which hated so much about talk*

It is interesting to observe the last sentence where the preposition is copied before the infinitive. This may be due to the influence of the French language; many French infinitives are preceded by *de*.

The first two sentences are different from the last one, namely, that the prepositions are copied after the infinitive. It indicates that once the meaning of the sentence is known, the subject produces a fronted prepositional phrase.

6.3.4.2 Nounless constructions

In the Grammaticality Judgements task all groups of learners produced more nounless phrases in relative than in non-relative constructions while the native speakers did just the opposite. Instead of using the native form, learners continue using full noun phrases not nounless constructions. In the study the following sentences were produced:

- las mujeres son aquellas que son dominantes – *women are those who are bossy*
- son las hermanas de la una que está casada – *are the sisters of the one that is married*
- ellos que han hecho esto deben ser ladrones – *they that have done that must be thieves*

The Spanish equivalent would be:

- las mujeres son <u>las</u> que son dominantes
- son las hermanas <u>de la que</u> está casada
- los <u>que</u> han hecho deben ser ladrones

These sentences are cases of nounless constructions.

6.3.4.3 Preposition copy

According to predictions this case does not belong to the nonnative grammar. It is noticeable that these are cases in which Spanish speakers do not copy the preposition but they produce such sentences like this:

- Es contigo que me casaré – *It is with you that I will marry.*

In the next sentence two out of five among the native speakers wrote *que* instead of *por lo que:*

- Era por eso por lo que no quería volver a verla.

  It was because of this <u>that</u> I did not want to see her again.

This rule does not belong to the learners' native grammar, only two students in the beginners' group follow this rule: one is of Greek origin and speaks Greek at home while the other is from Argentina who has a Spanish-speaking father.

6.3.4.4 Resumptive noun strategy

These are generally accepted by the students of the beginners' group and by the intermediate group to a certain extent. However, it is not really applied by the advanced and the control group which suggests that this strategy is not really the norm of the language. Sentences like these are frequently produced:

- Él (Peter) está aquí. – *He is here.*
- Hablaba de él (Peter). – *I was talking about him.*

On the other hand, students do not really produce sentences like these:

- Él está aquí (el libro). – *It is here.*
- Hablaba de él (el libro). – *I was talking about it (the book).*

The majority of students when translating *de él* referred to a person in the Grammaticality Judgements Task. The sentence like *"Debes venir porque ese problema de él que vamos a tratar de él es muy importante."* was translated by the majority of students as *"You must come because that problems of his that we are going to deal with is very important."*

Translations like the following are very rare:

> *"You must come because that problem that we are going to deal with is very important."*

In the blank-filling and translation tasks resumptive pronouns were produced with human and non-human antecedents both:

- El mozo que él lo contrató. – *The porter that he him hired.*
- No trabajaba lo bien que lo solía. – *He does not work as well that it used.*

In the first sentence *lo* refers to a human being while in the second sentence it could be the translation of *it*.

In the investigation there were three cases of resumptive pronouns which involved [+human] antedescentes. Two sentences were produced in compositions, one in the sentence combining task:

- Pero hay las personas <u>que para ellas</u> la punctualidad no existe.

  But there are persons <u>that for them</u> punctuality does not exist.

- Recibe a un forastero <u>que</u> no le conoce.

  He receives a foreigner <u>that</u> no him knows.

<u>Sentence combining task:</u>

- El locutor de quien vosotros estáis escuchando su voz.

  The announcer of whom you are hearing his voice.

Resumptive pronouns are hardly ever produced in English, however, they are perceived as possible Spanish constructions. In Spanish constructions nounless constructions are acceptable because they appear in other areas of grammar but they are rarely produced.

7. CONCLUSION

Since I was in the summer of 2001 in the United States, my experiences demonstrate that Hispanic, namely Spanish influence on the language of the country is increasingly stronger; especially in the southern states of the country, which once belonged to the territory of Mexico. The influx of the Mexican population to the northern states of the country is an even more remarkable peculiarity; even in the states of Indiana, Ohio or Illinois there are many bilingual advertisements, for example: *select-escoja.*

As I have written in my thesis, Mexican people are continuously going to the North in the hope of finding work or employment opportunity. Once, many centuries ago, the southern states were parts of the Mexican territory. From my experiences concerning my summer residence in the United States show that in the southern cities near the Mexican border for example in San Diego where the dominant language is Spanish, it is very rare to hear an English word.

Secondly, on the American continent the official language of the majority of countries is Spanish except for Canada (English-French bilingual country), Brasilia (Portuguese) and the United States. No wonder that in this way Spanish is so wide-spread in the United States, evenmore, in the whole world. Nowadays, as I can see, Spanish is the second most popular language in the whole world after English.

In the near future, according to me it is predictable and it can be imagined that one day the United States of America will become an English-Spanish bilingual country.

Printed in the United States
126132LV00004B/45/P